If you are a youth minister lc
actively involved in the ministry and to take on leadership
challenges, this is an indispensable guide.

—**Sean McDowell**, PhD
Speaker, writer, professor at Biola University, and author of
the Apologetics Youth Curriculum Advocates

Wow! This little book is packed with big, proven ideas that
will turn your youth into disciples and servants of Christ.
Tim Ramsey has been going beyond entertainment to
discipleship with his youth for years, and here he shares how
you can do the same. Get this book now!

—**Dr. Frank Turek**
Author, speaker, and radio host

Tim Ramsey has been one of the most influential people
I've known in my years of ministry. He has been a constant
encourager and friend for the past 16 years, and is always
available to listen and speak into my ministries. I've seen so
many people impacted by the vision and heart that Tim has
poured into student ministry. This book is a valuable resource
for anyone wanting to create a culture that equips students to
become servant leaders and world changers.

—**Micah Tyler**
Fair Trade Christian Artist, Dove Award nominee,
and songwriter

For years I have been encouraging youth leaders to deploy their students into the battlefield of ideas. Tim Ramsey provides the template for doing this, based on many years of experience as a youth pastor. If you want to transform your youth group for the better, get this book!

—J. Warner Wallace
Cold-case detective, Senior Fellow at the Colson Center for Christian Worldview, and author of *Cold-Case Christianity*, *God's Crime Scene*, and *Forensic Faith*

As a father of three students who have served with Tim in this ministry model, I can say it is truly amazing. As a committed Christian, father, and physician, I have also found this book to be extremely helpful in my own ministry, parenting my children, and even in my practice. The imperative transfer of ministry ownership in a believer's life needs to be done very well. This book will give the reader extremely valuable, practical application and encouragement on how to make that transfer. Anyone involved in parenting or ministry of any type, especially to young people, needs to read this book.

—Gregory C. McKeever, M.D.

GIVE THEM THE KEYS

Making a Youth Ministry
a *YOUTH'S* Ministry

TIM D. RAMSEY

LUCIDBOOKS

First Printing 2017

ISBN 10: 1632961350
ISBN 13: 9781632961358
eISBN 10: 1632961369
eISBN 13: 9781632961365

TABLE OF CONTENTS

Thank you to…

My incredible wife, Delia. Apart from my salvation, you are the greatest gift in my life. God uses you in so many ways to keep me going when I just don't think I can. You are such a tremendous example of what a true follower of Christ looks like. The way you serve our Savior and our family humbles and teaches me each day. I am so grateful for you.

My children (and grands), Christopher, Jessie, Carson, Ella, Zac, Melissa, Connor, Kailey, Jenna, and Brenton. You are such bright spots in my life. I am so encouraged to see how the Lord uses you and how you are serving Him. I love to spend time with you guys because, eventually, we will be laughing…hard!

All my students (past and present) at Fellowship. I have loved being your youth pastor for the last 25 years and I am looking so forward to what the Lord has for us to do together. It has been such an honor to get to be a part of your journey.

My pastor, C.F. I'll never forget you walking into my office all those years ago and handing me a CD of Dr. Ed Young Sr. to listen to about the importance of youth ministry in a church. Your support means more than I can say.

The board of One Road Ministries: Clint, David, and Greg. Thank you for your support, guidance, and accountability. I love you guys! Now let's go to breakfast!

Greg McKeever for your unwavering support and encouragement. I may not have ever finished this project without your prayers, prodding, and encouragement. Your weekly inquiries of, "Where are you at on your book?" and your constant "shots in the arm" by telling me to "Press On!" have meant more than I can say.

The Legacy of Wallace Shelton (Tom, Sharon, Lauren, and Tyler Fordyce). Your belief in what I do has made this moment possible. Thank you for allowing me the privilege of calling you guys, not just friends, but family!

My Pineywoods Camp family (Eric, Karla, Will, Pat, Steve, Diane, Jared, Banjo, Janel, and Katy). Thanks for all the days you let me come out and sit in your dining hall. Thanks for all the encouragement, for feeding me, and letting me write! You guys are unbelievable...also, just for the record, those hurricanes were NOT my fault!

BEST FOR LAST!
The Lord Jesus Christ for giving me new life, hope, and an unbelievable calling to ministry. You give me a reason to get up each day just so I can see what you are going to do that day. Lord, whatever I lay my hands to, may it flourish so that your Kingdom may be honored!

Chapter 1

WHY GIVE THEM THE KEYS?

When I was a teenager, my dad bought me a *very* used car. I remember that first drive by myself and how it felt, steering wheel in my hands and the hum of the engine in my ears as I showed all my friends. Trusting me with that car made me feel as if I had it all: freedom, value, and incredible responsibility. I was so excited to have that car that I spent two days polishing it until it shined. I kept it spotless inside and out. When the universal joint went out, I paid for the part and fixed it myself (quite the learning experience). With my part-time job, I made sure the car had gas and proper maintenance. That car was my baby, and I took care of it. It wasn't the newest or fastest, but it was mine to enjoy, and I loved it. It was a commitment that I loved having.

A few years ago, a student in my youth ministry called and wanted to come over and show my family her new car. It brought back memories of the excitement I had with my first car. She wanted the world to see what she had been entrusted with.

Have you ever noticed the mindset that comes when something valuable has been entrusted to you? It totally changes your perspective. You want to take care of it. You want to show it to your friends. You're willing to work for it because you feel responsible for it.

Entrusting ministry opportunities to our students has the same effect.

I have heard from many different sources that so many of our graduates are just not that committed to the local church after high school graduation. To those of us on the front lines of student ministry, that trend can be depressing, frustrating, and even defeating. Is there a way to change it?

As youth ministers, we are always on the lookout for the remedy to this situation, if it exists at all. Of course, it is through a relationship with Christ that hearts are changed and people come alive spiritually. It is the Holy Spirit who draws, guides, directs, convicts, and encourages us. It is the scripture that teaches and instructs us to become what God desires. But as youth ministers, we also need to look objectively at our ministries to see if what we do is building a strong Christian foundation or just a moral social club that makes great memories. We must make sure that we are fully utilizing our time with students and preparing them for the challenges they'll face outside the walls of the church and home.

Today many students are unprepared to face the world spiritually when they graduate from high school. Their core beliefs are challenged as they step out into the world. They have to take responsibility for what they believe and how these beliefs will affect their behavior. Often they're their own bosses for the first time and have freedom to choose what to do with their days—and their lives, for that matter.

Think about this upcoming change from a youth ministry perspective. A typical student who is involved in a youth ministry has been in the same place, around the same friends, with the same youth minister for several years. Then everything changes. He or she launches out into a new world, feeling disconnected from the norm. What once was a regular routine (school, friends, church) is diminished or gone altogether. Many students look for a new comfort zone. What will they find? While they are searching, will they have the correct focus?

Once in the world, students face professors, peers, and employers spouting anti-Christian rhetoric and touting their accolades to validate being an authority on these matters. Are students prepared to face this type of indoctrination? Have they been taught the truth of God's Word, and have they retained it?

Statistics reveal that students are increasingly choosing a more worldly path, one that will take them away from God and the church. What we as youth ministers impart to our students before they reach this point is crucial.

Unfortunately, I have heard people tell students (usually while shaking a finger at them), "You are the future leaders of the church. This is your time to prepare for future ministry." I respectfully challenge that statement. Students shouldn't be preparing for future ministry; they should be involved in ministry *now*, not later. Students want to serve, not sit. They yearn to discover a deeper purpose for their existence in the body of Christ in the present, not in the future.

Do students want to be entertained? Sure! But entertainment won't keep them connected in service to the body of Christ for a lifetime.

For many years, my youth ministry was solely event-driven. Yours may be as well. It's the model we've been practicing for years, the model we were told that parents and students wanted, and now we are reaping what we have sown.

In an event-driven ministry, students get hyped up for the upcoming event, but once it's over, the thrill is gone until the next big event. It's a year-long roller coaster ride. Consistency in attendance is difficult with this type of approach because students come for the events and bring their friends in droves, but where are all those students in between the big events?

Back then, I was teaching students that planning and executing ministry was my job, not theirs. I was teaching them to sit on the bench and wait for the "game" to begin. Students are trained to think, "If it's on my student ministry calendar, then I need to make sure that my 'ministry mode' is on; if it's not, then it's life as usual." It's the *usual* that we must change, because the *usual* is where students spend their time and make critical choices about their lives.

There are many great tools at our disposal as youth ministers—Bible studies, retreats, service opportunities, conferences, and camps, just to name a few. We plan and execute events, hoping that lives will be changed for the better, for the sake of the Kingdom. We can have incredible ministry activities, but the question we need to dwell on is this: How can we consistently effect change in the lives of our students if they do not show up consistently? Someone shared a statistic with me recently. It takes a minimum of one year of consistent discipleship to impact long-term change and commitment—not a six-week or even six-month discipleship program, but one solid year of consistent discipleship.

Let's face it. Today we struggle with the continuous battle of noncommittal Christianity. Often students attend a ministry with their boyfriend or girlfriend, best friend, or peer group. It's the relationship they care about, not the event, that makes them want to go to church. Where there is relationship, there is security and connection.

That isn't new information, but it's information we aren't using well. It's the relationship we have with our students and the relationship they have with each other that keep them coming back week after week. It's through our students' relationships outside the church that we gain the opportunity to affect more lives for the Kingdom of God. But it's not just a "bring them to the church" mentality; it's training our students that ministry is an everyday opportunity. If their focus is correct, then they are not only thinking about bringing their friends to church, but they're thinking about bringing their friends to Christ for a deeper, more meaningful relationship with Him.

Students must begin serving others for the sake of Christ. This occurs when they understand what the purpose of the Christian walk is all about. Just hearing about this purpose but never practicing it makes it more difficult to grasp. It's like signing up for a football team but never getting a chance to practice and play. If a coach leaves his team on the bleachers while he teaches them about the game and never puts them on the field, they'll know the playbook, but they'll start wondering, "What's the use of coming out here day after day and never being given the opportunity to play?" Aren't we doing the same thing as youth ministers when we don't allow our students to "get in the game?"

The ministry approach in this book is a fourfold approach:

1. Teach a student to look at his or her life as an important part of the Kingdom picture, in the here and now.

2. Train and equip each student for at least one specific ministry.

3. Release students to minister in their own ministries where they have ownership.

4. Reach students' peers through their ministry efforts, thus effecting change in them to eventually release them to minister as well.

This is how we begin to impact and change the *usual*. We teach our students that their self-worth is centered on who they are in Christ. By giving the students ownership of their ministries, we're giving them something tangible that will serve as a constant reminder of *whose* they are and their purpose in that relationship. Ministry ownership gives a sense of worth.

Their presence at ministry activities becomes more than just a ritual observance; it becomes something that has much deeper meaning and purpose. Giving students the authority of ministry responsibilities empowers them and communicates to them that they are being trusted with a very precious commodity. Suddenly they start taking pride in it. They want to make sure that it shines, that it's cared for, and that it runs well. They want to show their friends this precious commodity with which they've been entrusted.

Why Give Them the Keys?

When students have the opportunity to be more than spectators, they respond in amazing ways. This ministry approach is not just beneficial for the time they're students within the ministry, but also for when they are on their own. Instead of graduating and trying to find something that caters to them, they will pursue a new ministry to minister to and benefit the world around them.

This ministry approach gives students freedom, value, and incredible responsibility through ownership of their ministry. We simply need to give them the keys and let them drive.

Chapter 2

SOME OF THE BENEFITS
OF THIS MODEL

I had just asked a tenth grader to take the coordinator position of one of our ministry teams. He responded, "Are you serious? Oh yeah, baby, turn me loose!" To say the least, he was excited about it. The very next Wednesday at our midweek service, he was like a kid at Christmas. He is a very typical teenage guy, usually quiet and cool, but not that night. He was extremely enthusiastic, which was evident within his circle of friends. Some of those friends seemed a little uncomfortable, but most of them had caught his enthusiasm and were just as excited as he was.

Excitement of Ownership Breeds Enthusiasm

When students become excited about their ministries, enthusiasm multiplies. It's also a blast to watch a ministry grow from a single student and permeate through his or her peers. Another benefit of enthusiasm is that it has an effect on students' faith walks as well. When students are excited and enthusiastic about ministry, they talk about it. This excitement encourages them to talk about their faith, their ministry, and their youth group. One of the places that their enthusiasm is evident is on social media. These leaders and their team members are constantly posting things that are pointing people to Christ. The old saying that enthusiasm is contagious is a very true statement.

You want to see the enthusiasm continue. That's one reason to have monthly meetings with your students. We talk about the positive things we've seen God doing through their ministries. We also talk about their frustrations, and I always try to get them to look for new things to implement. We don't want them to get in a rut. Jack, my father-in-law, once told me that a rut was nothing more than a grave with no ends. A rut is an enthusiasm killer. So encourage students to dream often and to not be afraid to chase those dreams for their ministries. That keeps encouragement flowing. Students will often ask my opinion on an idea they have for their team. A student may ask, "Should we start a nursing home ministry or a veterans' recognition ministry?" My answer to them is "Yes!" They stand there and look a little bewildered; then I explain, "Do whatever your heart desires to do for the Lord and do it to the best of your ability!" A lot of times, they will still stand there, looking like I have lost every bit of sense I ever had. Then I explain in a very simple and direct manner, "It is your ministry, your vision, and your heart . . . do not limit both yourself and your ministry. Dream big!" I am not encouraging them to take on more than they can handle. I am simply helping them understand that there are no limits and that it is totally in their hands. Inevitably, when they understand that they have the ability and your backing to follow their vision for their ministry, enthusiasm explodes!

From Dependence to Confidence

One year we had a situation where several of our teams were not working well. Our leaders always had an excuse when asked why their teams weren't engaged in some sort of ministry activity. I constantly (and lovingly) asked what I or their Ministry Coach (Ministry Coach will be explained in the next chapter) could do to help them jump-start their teams. One of them finally confided that the main holdup for him was that he was afraid he might fail in some way.

We all know those students who allow fear to dictate their decisions. They sit back and wait for others to volunteer. Whether it's because of shyness, laziness, fear, or something else, they just sit back and wait for others to take the initiative. Acceptance from peers or the fear of losing that acceptance is probably the biggest reason students don't volunteer. They wonder, "What will my friends think?" or "What if my peers think that this is a 'lame' event and that's why no one else is volunteering?" or "What if I'm the only one who is going to do this and no one from my inner circle is there?" In a majority of cases, they are dependent on their friends for their self-worth. Those are some of my favorite students because when we can get them engaged, it's like watching a flower blossom. It's a thrill to see a student step out of the shadows and take on a leadership role within the ministry.

The beauty of this ministry model is that you will see it

time and time again. There will be what I like to call "turtle moments" when a student will step out and then, for some reason, step back into the shell. But don't be discouraged—at least they came out of their shell for a moment, and for some students that's a big step.

We must encourage our students and help them understand that it's their job to be obedient in service and that God brings the results. I always remind my students of a few things in the Bible that show us how that looks. Noah built the ark, but it was God who shut the ark's door and saved them. Abraham left his homeland on God's command, and God blessed him for his obedience, making him the father of a great nation. Moses stood up to Pharaoh, and God blessed him by making him one of the greatest spiritual leaders. Paul followed the calling of the Lord, and the Lord did amazing things through him, making him one of the greatest apostles.

It's about helping our students see that it's not about what they are able to do by their own power and abilities. It's about trusting what God can do through their abilities when they walk in obedience. When a student begins to truly understand that the only thing that's expected of them is obedience to serve our Lord in their ministries, you'll see their confidence begin to grow. At one of our monthly meetings at my home, we shared a meal and talked about life, sports, the newest apps, and Clash Royale tactics (I don't play CR, but I nod my head like I know what they are talking about). I asked them to bring their goals for their ministries to the meeting. As each one told me his or her goals, I could see that most of them hadn't really thought through their goals before. Once we'd gone around the room, I told them to make an "X" over the goals that they had written down. I explained that their goals, for the most part, were good goals, but not their priority. I then instructed them to write down "Be obedient." We then looked at Hebrews 11 and the kind of people God uses. That chapter lists the great people of faith and reveals that through their *obedience*, God did amazing things. Some still had doubts and concerns when we parted company that night. The next night, at our midweek service, one of the students who was at the meeting said to me, "I finally understand what you mean when you say 'God doesn't care *what* we do for him. He cares about *why* we do it.' I don't have to be the best; I just have to be obedient, and he'll do the rest." He set aside his fear from that moment on, and his ministry team became alive.

It's important that students gain confidence, not in themselves but in the One they are serving. When that happens, a whole new world opens up for them.

Train Students to Look for Ministry, Not Wait for It to Find Them

Several years ago, a new student to our ministry and to the faith approached me and asked when I was going to schedule our next ministry event. We had just come back from a missions trip, and she wanted to be part of more ministry activities. I explained our ministry teams to her and how she could be involved in ministry all the time. She didn't jump in right away, but eventually she joined a team, and by her senior year, she was leading a team. She was always asking me and others in our community if there were projects that she and her team could be part of. She was consistently on the prowl for ministry opportunities. After graduation, she was home for Christmas, and I had a chance to chat with her.

I asked her about her first semester and what she thought of it. She told me about her classes, grades, and favorite professors, but then she told me about an after-school ministry she had joined. The ministry was prepping her to lead a group for the upcoming semester. I asked her how long she had been part of that ministry. She said that once she got to school, she started checking out the ministry opportunities in her area and then decided to try the one she was telling me about.

Once she got settled at college, she didn't hesitate to find a new ministry. She was conditioned and trained to look for her ministry. She didn't sit back, wait for it to find her, and then put on the ministry mindset. The mindset/heartset was already in place, and she just continued the journey as a servant in a new location.

One Size Fits All

Last year, my family and I got together and rented a beach house for a weekend getaway. One night we went onto the nearby island for dinner and shopping. In one of the stores, I found a hat that I really liked. The tag on the inside of the hat read "One Size Fits All." After trying it on, I realized that statement was not true. There is always a sense of frustration when I try on an item that is the magical "one size fits all," only to find out that I do not fit into the category of "all." You might also be a little cautious about whether there is a ministry model that can fit every ministry size. The beauty of the ministry model I propose in this book is that you can easily tailor it to meet the size and needs of any student ministry.

One of the first steps you'll want to take is to find out your students' strengths and likes. Help them develop and focus their energies there. Be sure you are helping them develop ministry focuses that are theirs and not what you think they should be. We'll talk more about student development later in the book.

As you read this book, beware of a danger that could creep in. Make sure you keep your focus on the students you have and not on the students you wish you had. I am not talking about the number of students but about the gifting and interests your current students have. We sometimes look around at other student ministries and see what they have and wonder "what if?" A former pastor of mine, Larry Petton, once told me to never compare my student ministry to another. He said, "You'll either be prideful or jealous, and both are deadly." So as you go through this book, focus solely on *your* students and their abilities.

You Can Make It Your Own

One thing I have learned in student ministry is that there are very, very few new ideas. It really has all been done before, just with different packaging. Solomon said in Ecclesiastes 1:9 that there is nothing new under the sun. This ministry approach is nothing new; I am just sharing what and how we do it. You can use this as a guideline, but I urge you to make your own. Youth groups are different and diverse. One of the things I love about traveling and speaking to different youth groups around the country is seeing the diversity within and among the groups. It is so much fun to get to know the students and talk to them about their lives, their joys, their fears, and their faith. I have learned so much in these conversations. One of the biggest things I see and recognize is that we are all not the same. We have the same Savior, yes, but we are different in so many ways. I also extremely enjoy getting to know the youth workers, finding out where they are on their journeys. I love what I can learn from them as well. I get to see all sorts of different youth ministry approaches, but at their very root, they are all the same.

I get great ideas from observing other youth leaders. In some cases, I take the things I see being done and tweak them a bit so they fit the needs of my youth ministry. I was speaking at a youth winter retreat in the Pocono Mountains a few years ago. The last event of the weekend was a snow sledding competition, which was a tradition of this annual retreat. The students from all the youth ministries there built sleds out of cardboard and duct tape. The categories for judging were the most creative, the most artistic, the best slide form, the fastest, and the one that went the farthest. The event was so much fun to watch. My favorite moment was when two competitors, who had both built cardboard tanks, raced at the same time while firing potato guns at each other. I was having so much fun watching this that I almost missed my flight home.

I wanted to do that, but in the part of Texas where I live, snow is extremely rare (in fact, the only white stuff we can count on is under the trees at Walmart), so I tweaked it and made it fit our group. We had a raft-building contest at our next winter retreat. Our students had to build a raft with the items supplied (duct tape, rope, 1x4s, and three car tire inner tubes). They had to take their rafts and race out into the lake, around a particular spot that was marked, and then back. The image of that moment still makes me laugh—especially the team who's inner tube lost all its air during the race!

Some of the Benefits of This Model

But the bottom line is taking ideas and making them fit your ministry. If this is a ministry approach you'd like to implement in your youth ministry, then tweak it and make it yours. Nobody is going to know your students and your ministry like you do, so take it and make it fit your students and your ministry. Once you do, don't be surprised when there is a new excitement that takes over your group. It's amazing to watch.

Chapter 3

PROPOSING THE VISION

I love the final scene in the old movie *Indiana Jones and the Last Crusade*. The Joneses (Indiana and his father, Henry Sr.), Marcus Brody, and Sallah all mount their horses to ride off, and Marcus shouts, "Henry! Follow me, I know the way. Hyaaah!" and spurs his horse and clumsily races off. Then Henry looks at Indiana and says, with a sense of skepticism, "Got lost in his own museum, huh?"

Sometimes people look at us like that—very skeptically—when we propose something new. In this chapter, we are going to look at proposing the vision to your adult leaders first.

Change is something that makes a lot of people uncomfortable, especially if they perceive that it means they possibly may have to work a little more to do it. But remember, just as we said in the last chapter, enthusiasm is contagious.

Also, depending on the number of ministry teams you start, you may not need a lot of outside adult help. Let me encourage you that no matter how many you start with, it's always a good idea for student leaders/ministers to have adult volunteers available and informed about the overall goal of this ministry approach. As this new ministry endeavor grows, you will already have in place adults to whom you can hand off the baton. Adults who serve as volunteers in this model are called Ministry Coaches, which are a must if we are to see this ministry model reach its full potential. When properly focused and trained, these coaches will be able to "keep the train on the tracks" for each ministry team. They will wear many hats in this role. They are instructors, teachers, cheerleaders, encouragers, mentors, and accountability coaches, but they must be constantly reminded that they are *not to be the leader.*

Let me explain that last part. It is in my nature to take over when I perceive something is not going as I would like. Many of you know what I am talking about. Within this ministry model, we do battle at times with all sorts of desires to take over certain situations. Of course, that is counter to the overall focus of this ministry model. So proper training for our Ministry Coaches is imperative. We will talk more about that in just a bit.

From my experience, skepticism from adult leaders will be your first hurdle. In all my years of using this ministry model, most of the skepticism comes from my most devoted workers—the ones who are at every event and who do a majority of the work. Because these devoted saints are always on the front lines, they feel an obligation to fulfill the needs that they hear about. Be careful allowing these volunteers to take on too much. It could cause burnout or a half-hearted approach to their ministry team. One amazing aspect of this ministry model is that it gives potential adult volunteers an opportunity to come off the sidelines and join the game. It's important to understand that these adults don't have to be the coolest or the most popular, but they do have to truly love the Lord and love students.

The skeptics of this ministry model are typically skeptical because they think, for the most part, that students are not ready or able to fulfill what's necessary to make a ministry successful. In some ways, they are correct. The experience level of our students is not the same as older, more mature, and experienced adults. But that's why there is training, mentoring, and encouraging that has to take place. The old approach of teaching someone how to swim by throwing them into a body of water doesn't always turn out well. My brother jumped into a pool as a child before he knew how to swim and had to be pulled out by someone who knew how to swim. Our parents eventually put us in swimming lessons, and we all learned how to swim. After that, my brother could jump in and swim. Training our students is part of what we do. Our adults need to be reminded that we are all called to serve, no matter our age or experience.

As older and more mature believers, we are to use our gifts to prepare our students and release them to minister. Look at Ephesians 4:11–12:

> *And he gave the apostles, the prophets, the evangelists, the shepherds and teachers,* to equip the saints *for the work of ministry, for building up the body of Christ* (emphasis added).

This passage makes it very clear that there are people whose gift is the responsibility to train up the body of Christ for service.

Adult volunteers in student ministry have the privilege of teaching, training, and preparing this generation of students. Because we are training them to live out their faith according to scripture, we are placed in the gifted category. It is our job as leaders of youth ministries to teach and train each of these volunteers. Bible teachers, music leaders, cooks, van drivers, vomit cleaners (which are very necessary and appreciated when that certain Wednesday night game gets out of hand), and others are all training students. They are training them directly and indirectly through the spoken word and through visible actions.

Types of Adult Volunteers

In many cases, you will typically encounter one of five types of adult volunteers:

1. The Over-Reacher

2. The Last-Minute Volunteer

3. The Vapor Volunteer

4. The Armchair Quarterback

5. The Tentmaker

Let's look at each one and see how we can help them reach their full potential. In all actuality, sometimes we don't have a lot of choices when it comes to volunteers. With each of these, I will offer ways to help you mold them, if possible, into great Ministry Coaches.

The Over-Reacher

We always have within our ministries those individuals I like to call "Over-Reachers," or in other words, "control freaks." The positive side of these types of potential leaders is the drive they have. When properly focused, Over-Reachers are our go-getters when we need things accomplished. But when it comes to helping and enabling students to lead a ministry, they can struggle. If not reined in, they can kill the enthusiasm of a student who is trying to lead a ministry, so proceed cautiously.

I have had my share of over-reacher volunteers over the years. From my experience, the best thing to do with these types of individuals is to ease them slowly into a leadership position. I try my best not to immediately put them in charge of a ministry team. Giving them small tasks helps them focus on serving. A lot of times, when these personalities are not given immediate authority, they will eventually leave to find a ministry in which they can take ownership. But if they stick around, that's a great sign that they are willing to submit and learn. Typically, you'll never see all their desire to control disappear completely, but if they are conditioned properly and held accountable, they will make great Ministry Coaches.

The Last-Minute Volunteer

During the American Revolutionary War, the Minute Men were trained and ready to be deployed at a moment's notice. We have volunteers who sit on the sidelines and hear the needs of the student ministry, but they wait to be personally "called up" into service at the last minute—thus the term

Last-Minute Volunteer. These individuals usually say things like this: "Well, if you can't find anyone else . . ."

The positive element in this kind of volunteer is that he or she is almost always willing to serve, but just not interested in total commitment. There can be many different reasons why they are hesitant—insecurity, laziness, hectic schedules, pride—but it holds them back. Everyone has a desire to be needed, so a great approach for these individuals is to let them know that they are always needed. Encouraging and reminding them that they are needed will hopefully invoke a stirring within them to get up, take part, and stay involved. This type of volunteer is a little more high maintenance, but because of their drive, they can make great Ministry Coaches. Once they are involved, keep on encouraging them—this is a must! From my experience with these types of volunteers, once they know they are appreciated and needed, they will usually charge the battlefield.

The Vapor Volunteer

One of the best things I learned early on in my ministry career was to delegate. It was a difficult thing to do because I struggled with setting very specific standards that were so high that nobody but I could attain them, or so I thought. Eventually I learned to give out responsibilities and let my volunteers put their own spin on things.

To be successful, I had to learn to delegate, but there are some volunteers who make it very difficult. I like to call them Vapor Volunteers. They are there for a moment, and then, just as you turn around, poof! they're gone, often leaving you holding the bag. Those who have been around student ministry long enough have all encountered the Vapor Volunteer.

I have had buses not show up on the day of events only to find out that the Vapor Volunteer never lined them up. I've gone to pick up our curriculum for a discipleship weekend and found it was never submitted to our printing company. The list goes on and on.

My other problem is that I err on the side of grace. I always want to give others a second (or third, fourth, and maybe even fifty-seventh) chance. It just comes down to a spiritual maturity issue on their part. In all honesty, there is not a lot you can do for these individuals except pray for them and maybe offer them a discipleship opportunity. In my opinion, these are the types of volunteers you do not want to be Ministry Coaches. Until they can show that they can stick to their commitments, keep them out of that position.

The Armchair Quarterback

I love college football, especially watching the Texas A&M Aggies play (don't be hatin'...God loves us all!). My youngest son, Brenton, and I go to the home games or watch them on Saturdays with great excitement. If you're a fan of football, you know how it feels to be better quarterbacks in the stands or on the couch than the ones on the field. My son and I used to say things like, "Wow! What was he thinking? He had a guy wide open in the end zone! Oh, c'mon!" Sound familiar?

Sometimes we critique and pick apart other people's work without even thinking about it. The sad thing is, I know that I am nowhere near the athlete that those collegiate athletes are, but I sit in my recliner, watching and offering advice to my television screen as if that's going to help the situation.

We have those types of individuals within our volunteer corps as well. We don't see them actually leading as volunteers, but we do hear from them quite often, usually when something didn't go as planned. In some cases, it may seem that in some way they want to benefit from our mishaps or they feel they are helping us by pointing out the obvious. Whatever the case, we usually don't appreciate it much. What I have learned to do with these types of volunteers is ask them to be in charge of the area where the mishap took place last time. I have been pleasantly surprised that most of the time, they accept the responsibility. What's even better is when they do a good job handling that task. Now there are those who try to take our shortcomings and use them against us. It is those people that typically do not fit the Ministry Coach description. The last thing we need is a Ministry Coach telling the student leadership where they have failed, completely with the wrong purpose in mind. Those are the volunteers I call Armchair Quarterbacks. But on the other side of the coin, there are Armchair Quarterbacks who will point out our shortcomings with the right kind of heart—a heart that is trying to help us follow the Lord. Some of those conversations are very humbling, but if we receive them with the correct heart, they can make us even better for the work of the ministry.

(Sidenote: Don't always put people in this category just because they bring up something negative. We all have our shortcomings, and some of those are blind spots. Listen with an open heart to see what the Lord may be teaching you.)

The Tentmaker

Every now and again, that special volunteer comes along who must have trained under the apostle Paul himself. They just want to serve. They do not look for the spotlight and in many cases avoid it at all costs. These are the perfect Ministry Coaches. I call these types of volunteers the Tentmakers.

The apostle Paul supported himself as a tentmaker. He didn't want others to support him because he thought it might detract from the gospel. These amazing volunteers are not dependent upon others to keep them in the game. They also do not want anything they do to detract from the focus of the ministry endeavor.

They are also like the Energizer Bunny—they just keep going, and going, and going! Now let's face it, these types of volunteers are a rare commodity, but they do exist. Once you find volunteers like that, make sure you keep them encouraged by sending them notes of gratitude and doing little acts of kindness for them. They typically will shy away from a public show of appreciation, but a very occasional moment of recognition will bless them and remind them that they are not taken for granted. These are ideal Ministry Coaches, but like I said, they are not always easy to find.

Recruitment

Once a year at my church, I host a student ministry parent and volunteer dinner. The purpose of the dinner is to build relationships with the parents of students who are new to the ministry, reinforce established relationships with parents of current students, and encourage my volunteers. After dinner, we share a video of the past year's activities and provide a verbal summary of all that has been accomplished. We then turn our focus to the upcoming programs and events of our student ministry year. During that time, I expound on the ministry teams and explain each of them. I also explain what Ministry Coaches are and where they, as parents and volunteers, could plug into this ministry opportunity. In all honesty, I've never experienced a rush of people wanting to volunteer, but I do have a lot of inquiries. I take note of those who are truly interested and make a point to follow up with them over the next couple of weeks.

Once you begin the process of recruiting volunteers, you'll need to find out what the motivation is for their involvement. It's important to understand that this is an interview process. You want to make sure they fit the ministry mold that you need. This can be done over coffee, lunch, or even a laid-back office visit. Here are a few questions you can ask a prospective volunteer:

- What's your daily spiritual journey like?
- Why do you want to do this?
- What are your goals and what do you want to see happen through your involvement?
- What kind of approach are you planning on using (mentoring, encouraging, daily floggings . . .)?
- Do you think you are patient enough for this kind of ministry?
- Are you able to allow students to fail and not get frustrated?
- Are you able to take the necessary time to invest in student leadership?

The most important thing you are looking for in a Ministry Coach is an adult who is a very committed Christ follower.

These are the individuals who are constantly in the scripture and trying their best to live it out. Seriously, would you ask a person to coach a sports team who doesn't continually study the game in order to be better at it? Just having a desire and an interest to be involved doesn't qualify someone to be a volunteer.

So, to put it simply, don't rush in! Having the wrong person take this position can be devastating. I know all too well! Make sure these coaches know that the relationship with their student ministry leader is key. As noted before, relationships are key for trust, and trust is needed so the leader will follow the instructions and the teachings.

One final, extremely important detail is that the Ministry Coach must understand that you, as the ministry head, are still the overall leader of the ministry. You have the final say in all things. Recruiting the right Ministry Coaches is the first building block in putting all the pieces together for this ministry approach. Make sure the ministry leaders have a good coach in place to ensure that they are successful, because you cannot be successful in this model without quality Ministry Coaches.

Chapter 4

PROCLAIMING THE MESSAGE

As a long-time youth minister, one of the cool things I get to be part of is performing the weddings of former students, along with the premarital counseling leading up to the wedding. One of the main items we discuss in the counseling sessions is the importance of proper communication. Communication is imperative to a healthy relationship. Good communication builds trust and friendship within a relationship. Verbalizing expectations, communicating joys and frustrations, setting goals, and planning the future together are things that need to be communicated so the couple can establish a solid foundation. When you lack communication, a lot of problems can arise. But when good communication is in place, it can certainly help take out almost all the guesswork.

With this ministry model, you need to communicate to

students so they understand what is expected. You cannot successfully recruit students if they do not understand the *why, what, where, when,* and *how* of this ministry. These are very easy to explain. Let's take a few moments to look at them.

The *Why*

Here's the *why* of this ministry model—and this is a simple one (say the answer in your best Forrest Gump voice): "Because Jesus said to." There are so many verses that remind us that we are called to serve. In Mark 9:35, Jesus told the disciples, "Whoever wants to be first must be last of all and servant of all" (NRSV). The word *servant* in this verse, in its original language, is *diákonos.* It is from this word that we get our word *deacon.* It describes one who attends to the needs of others freely and not as a slave who has no choice. It means we as followers of Christ choose to serve because we want to, not because we have to. The opportunity to serve is a gift that all believers have been given. The apostle Paul wrote in Galatians 5:13:

> *For you were called to freedom, brothers. Only do not use your freedom as an opportunity for the flesh, but through love serve one another.*

God gives us the ability to live our lives as we choose, but one of His desires is for us to serve Him while serving others.

This ministry model is not just about serving; it's about what is accomplished through serving. We serve in order to share the gospel and to be the gospel. People will know that we are true followers of Jesus by our love—the love that we live out every day for our Heavenly Father and also the love that we share with those around us. The old saying is still true today that the best sermon ever preached was the one in tennis shoes. In other words, it is a life that is dedicated to living obediently to Christ that is a walking gospel tract. As we teach our students to serve with the heart of Christ, they are, by their example, preaching the gospel.

Another reminder for students is the Judgment Seat of Christ. There are those churches that avoid the word *judgment*. Our church does not (another reason I love our church and my pastor). But you have to understand that we are not painting a picture of gloom and doom, but rather of truth, hope, and encouragement. That's what the Judgment Seat of Christ does for the believer—it brings truth, hope, and encouragement. If we can help our students properly understand the Judgment Seat of Christ, then we can help them be on their guard against sin and indifference. As their leaders, counselors, and encouragers, we truly understand that the sin and indifference we experience in this life can rob us of our desire to serve our Savior. Our students need to truly grasp that if they turn themselves over to sin and indifference, their life will never reach the full potential that the Lord desires for them. We are all allotted a specific number of days that we are to redeem for God's glory. That is why Paul exhorts us in Ephesians 5:15–16:

> *Be very careful, then, how you live—not as unwise but as wise, making the most of every opportunity, because the days are evil* (NIV).

If we allow sin and indifference to creep in, we pass up God-given opportunities to serve Him, opportunities in which we would otherwise perform and for which we would otherwise be rewarded. Teaching the *why* to your students is the first starting block.

What's the *What?*

Let me put it this way, the *what* is the simple and the impossible. When I first started using this ministry model, it was my inclination to encourage our student leaders to start slowly. I assumed that if they encountered struggles, they would lose heart and pull away from their ministry. What I learned was that failure was a great teacher. I love the scene in the Disney movie *Meet the Robinsons* where the main character, Lewis, tries to repair the peanut butter and jelly gun only to have it explode. Instead of being barraged by complaints and taunts, he is met with cheers. In that moment, someone says, "From failing you learn, from success . . . not so much."[1] I always remind my students that failure isn't truly a failure unless you quit, and that failure is not the opposite of success but rather a part of it. With this in mind, however, don't ever limit your students' dreams or desires. Encourage them instead. Sometimes the dreams they have for their ministries may seem impossible to attain, but encourage them to chase what they know is something only God can do. We never want to teach our students to go after only what is humanly attainable. A student who was the ministry team coordinator for our recreation ministry had the daunting task of planning recreation for our Youth Week (a type of

---

1. *Meet the Robinsons*, directed by Stephen J. Anderson, Walt Disney Animation Studios, 2007.

day camp we do every summer). This particular year we had an extraordinary number of students. This ministry team coordinator planned a recreation that was very involved, and he needed a lot of assistance from our adults. I looked at the situation and thought it would be an uphill battle to make it successful. What he had planned was what he had dreamed, and he never wavered. There were a few moments when I could see the stress on his face (I also had a backup plan in place, just in case—and I know what you are thinking: "O ye of little faith"[2]). He knew that recreation during Youth Week was extremely important, but he kept his focus, we kept encouraging him, and it was a great success.

Where's the *Where?*

So where's the *where?* Simple—it is everywhere and anywhere. Challenge your students to think outside the box . . . or better said, outside the four walls of our churches. Jesus did just that when He charged the disciples in Matthew 28:19–20 to "Go therefore and make disciples of all nations." In Acts 1:8, Jesus reiterated His desire for them to go wherever possible to share the gospel: "and you will be my witnesses in Jerusalem and in all Judea and Samaria, and to the end of the earth." Challenge your students to define where Jerusalem, Judea, Samaria, and the ends of the earth are in their personal world; then release them to go to these places. When you encourage them to look outside their comfort zone, you give them the opportunity to let great things happen in their spiritual journeys.

---

2. Matthew 6:30 (KJV).

One way the *where* has become tangible to our students has been through special speakers. We have had numerous local ministers and foreign missionaries come and speak at our church over the years. As they share their stories, the students find their *where*. Because of these moments, our students begin to look outside the walls of the church for ministry opportunities. I have had numerous students plan their own foreign missions trips. After one of the first of these missions trips, I felt a little threatened (just being honest). I felt that the church might look at the situation and say, "Why are you here, and why are we paying you?" I felt I had to be part of the planning so it would seem as if the youth minister was in control. I realized that it was my insecurity wanting me to be part of it so I could be viewed as the one behind this missions endeavor, thus making me look good. I had to work through those insecurities because if I didn't, I was working against what this ministry model was supposed to be about—the students taking the lead and making it their own. These students did not wait for permission (even though they did talk to me and their parents at the beginning) or for someone else to plan the trip for them; they just stepped out and made it happen. They made it happen, but it will not happen if we do not help them understand the *where* of ministry opportunities.

When's the *When?*

When is the *when*? It's the here and now. We can always come up with a reason not to do something. Procrastination is a killer, and it usually will creep in when students think a particular task is just too big and doubt takes over. I have had students who, because of doubting their own abilities, try to accomplish only small tasks. Please understand that there is nothing small or insignificant when it comes to the overall spectrum of working for our Father's Kingdom. The point is that we shouldn't limit ourselves to small tasks out of fear.

Another struggle you will encounter is the struggle of the calendar. Students today are overwhelmed at times with life. Whether it's school, sports, jobs, relationships (inside and outside the family unit), or electronic distractions—the list can go on and on. We need to help them know that there is a small window of time that the Lord gives us to be here on the earth. I have a friend, Paul, who attends our church. For years he served on a disaster mortuary operational response team. He served in New York City after the attack on September 11, 2001, and was also called on when the Space Shuttle *Columbia* disintegrated over Texas in 2003. Several years ago, I asked him how he handled death on that level. He took a piece of paper and drew a long horizontal line and then drew two short vertical lines on each end. On one end of the line he wrote birth, and on the other end he wrote death. He handed me the pen and said, "Mark on this timeline where you think your life is at this moment." I pondered, shrugged my shoulders, and then marked it somewhere in the middle. Then he took the pen and pointed to a place on the line that was near the beginning. "Most teenagers mark way over here," he said. But then he drew an arrow at the portion of the line that is just before the part that said "death" and said, "This is how I live my life. Death is a guarantee, and we are not promised tomorrow, so I know what I am dealing with is part of our life here. I also want to be mindful to live my life in a way that makes a difference and counts." Even though much time has passed, those words still resonate within me, and I often remind my students to redeem their time (Ephesians 5:16).

But *How?*

This is the fun part. We as youth ministers get to teach the *how* of our students' ministries. We get to pour into them and eventually watch them pour into others. We know from experience that the *how* is done in and through God's power and our willingness to be used. The focus is not just to condition them to some sort of mindless activity, but to train them to be Kingdom-focused in all they do. The *how* is really a blank canvas that you give them. One of the things I love to see is students who take over a ministry and bring in new and fresh ideas of their own. They don't feel as if they need to carry the same kind of torch for their ministry that their predecessor carried. Every year as we prepare to launch our new ministry teams, I always remind the leaders that the canvas is blank and they can do whatever they want. I encourage them to pray and seek what the Lord is leading them to do and also spend time investigating all sorts of opportunities. This is also the time that I will remind or inform them of the freedom they have to create their masterpiece. But the point is not to just think about what you want to paint, but to start putting paint on the canvas. In other words, get going!

That Aha! Moment

I have had students move to our city who were very active in their past church's youth ministry. Coming into our ministry, some were a little taken back by the amount of responsibility our students have and also how students were encouraged to serve, not just sit. To some, it was uncomfortable because they felt as if there were demands on them (we are always very careful not to come across as if we are pressuring them to serve on a team; it is simply an opportunity we offer). In a lot of cases, something clicks, and they finally understand the vision of our ministry. They experience this Aha! moment. Helping students have that Aha! moment and catch the vision is a major goal. Students need to grasp and embrace the *why, what, where, when,* and *how* of ministry if they are going to be committed to serving in this capacity. When this realization takes place, they see themselves in a new light, which is so worthwhile.

Chapter 5

DRIVER'S ED (STUDENT LEADER RECRUITMENT)

As a youth minister, I longed for years to see my students step up and lead. For me, that was the sign of maturity in their lives that I was hoping for. It would prove that the ministry was successful in its endeavor to train and encourage students to lead for the cause of Christ. Over the years, though, I realized I was not providing adequate opportunities for our students to step up and lead. This chapter should be a point of reference for you as a youth minister and for your Ministry Coaches.

Several years back, our student ministry hosted a lock-in. The students were divided into teams for various challenges and competitions. One part of the evening was called a "cooking war" (this was definitely pre-Iron Chef—I was ahead of my time and didn't realize it!). It was a blast watching them create and cook.

Give Them the Keys

When the time was up, the teams had to present their creations to the judges. I noticed that nearly all the teams had one student who stepped up to lead this endeavor. They orchestrated the delegation of the responsibilities and oversaw the entire team's activities. But there was one team that did not have a student step up to take the lead. They struggled and argued, and when their entry was submitted, well, it was pretty bad. That night the team entries were nearly burnt egg rolls, some sort of greenish hamburger helper, grilled peanut butter and jelly and pear sandwiches, and something with noodles and tuna. It was not the best presentation of culinary skills, but we, as judges, bravely tasted everything.

The students worked so hard on their dishes, and they were proud of their entries. By the end of the judging, we declared the first place dish (the egg rolls, by the way), and everybody got to enjoy all the entries. I noticed that the students who asked if we were enjoying their dish were the ones who had taken ownership during the competition. There was a sense of pride in what they'd accomplished, not only in their finished product but also in their team. They loved being the chef more than being the restaurant patron. It reminded me of when my dad had handed me the keys to my very first car—it was the thrill of driving all on my own. Years later, I remembered that night at the lock-in and those students who "took the keys" and got their teams where they wanted them to go. The thought occurred to me, along with some conviction, that I was spoon-feeding my students instead of letting them be the chef.

The success of this ministry model hinges on several factors. But none are more important than this one factor: without the right student leaders, the ministry team is nothing more than a rudderless ship. Please let me interject one thing. Long before you begin the recruitment process, you need to be in constant prayer for your students and Ministry Coaches. For me, the prayer is simple: ask God to raise up students for leadership and place upon their hearts a desire to serve Him and others. This is paramount because I cannot know the heart, and I am dependent upon Him to bring the right students forward.

Once you begin the process of recruiting your student leaders, do not hurry the process. A hurried process can create a lot of frustration, both on your part and on theirs. When you are ready to begin the process, make sure you spend time helping the students understand fully what this ministry approach is all about. At the beginning, I don't make any announcements that I am looking for leaders, but rather that I am looking for servants. I will usually teach a Bible study series during our Wednesday night youth service on the biblical example and definition of being a servant. The last study in this series will deal with being a servant leader and the qualifications of that position. It is at this point that I unfold before them the need for student leaders and explain fully what that entails.

We have an application that each candidate for leadership must complete and turn in. Even those students who have led a team for us in the past must fill out this application again. On that application is a list of what they are committing to do. On the last page, there is a place for the students to sign as well as a place for their parents to sign. Parents need to understand what their children are committing to from the start.

Make sure you put a firm deadline in place for the applications. That deadline has shown me so many times which students are really interested and committed and which ones are not. Once the applications are submitted to me, we begin the interviews. Once the interviews are completed and every candidate has been interviewed, I set up a second meeting with each candidate and inform them of my decision. At this meeting, I always have a youth ministry assistant or Ministry Coach with me just so nothing I say can be misunderstood or misused outside of that meeting.

Now that your leaders are in place, it's time to teach them how to "drive." I have never encountered a student who was perfectly ready to take over a team. I have been close a time or two, but at this stage they aren't completely ready. What I do at this point is take our new and returning student leaders on a summer retreat. That is where they will learn what it means to have the keys of the ministry. This intentional training time is more important than I can stress, because this is where their real understanding takes place. As a team, we experience great times of teaching, training, prayer, and enjoying community with each other. We have a pretty intense schedule during this retreat, but we also take time out to have some fun.

It's during this retreat that we challenge our leaders to dream big. We discuss possible roadblocks that could inhibit the success of their ministries. One of the main struggles I encounter with these leaders is self-doubt or apprehension. There are a lot of reasons for their apprehension. Their concerns range from a fear of what their peers may think to a fear of failure, a fear of commitment (or overcommitment), a fear of not being good enough, a fear of having to lead adults at times, and even a fear of the unknown. The list could be longer. During the retreat, I have them identify their areas of interest, abilities, and gifting. I always bring the conversation around to focus on their gifting and break down 1 Peter 4:10–11, which has these amazing words:

As each has received a gift, use it to serve one another, as good stewards of God's varied grace: whoever speaks, as one who speaks oracles of God; whoever serves, as one who serves by the strength that God supplies—in order that in everything God may be glorified through Jesus Christ. To him belong glory and dominion forever and ever. Amen.

These verses are such an encouraging and challenging portion of scripture. They apply not only to a limited spectrum of our ministry teams but also to our Christian lives as a whole. Take a look:

1. Every believer has received a gift of some sort.

2. We are commanded (not suggested) to use it to serve others and not be selfish with this gifting.

3. If we do not use it properly, we are not being good stewards of God's blessing of this gift.

4. God will always provide the tools we need.

5. If we use our gifting correctly, then God receives the glory.

I love it when students grasp the immensity of these two verses—five simple but powerful truths that show us how to focus as ones who are called to serve Him unconditionally. They're also great verses to share in the overall recruitment of ministry team members and can be such an amazing encouragement and challenge for your leaders. If we help them grasp this incredible truth, we'll help them save themselves so much strain and struggle. They need to know that they are commanded and capable of doing great things for our Lord, but they have to let the Lord use them in their gifting for His work. Instilling confidence within them will make the next step much easier to attain.

Next, you must get them excited about serving. Remember, enthusiasm is contagious. If you as the youth minister are genuinely excited about their strengths, abilities, and desires, then they will be, too. Their enthusiasm blossoms once they grasp their calling and believe that you really have confidence in them to lead. As their youth minister, it's incredible to see this amazing transformation take place as your students take the keys.

Help Them Understand Their *Present* Importance

During our retreat, either I or an adult leader teaches students to look at their lives as an important part of the Kingdom picture. Remember the story I shared with you earlier about the person who told the students they were to be the *future* leaders? When we look at 1 Peter 4:10, it reminds us that we are to be using our gifts now for the glory of God: "As each has received a gift, use it to *serve one another,* as good stewards of *God's varied grace*" (emphasis added). There is not any connotation to age, but only that believers have received the ability and the charge to use that ability for God. It's important to understand the word *steward.* A steward was one who served as the master's house manager. Historically, he had no money or possessions of his own, but he had to handle his master's wealth according to his master's will and instruction. So to sum up this verse, our students, as believers, are given abilities and gifts that they are to use to serve one another. Our Heavenly Master has bestowed these gifts upon us, and we must not let them sit idle. If we do not use them, we are not being good stewards. Remember the parable of the talents in Matthew 25:14–30? Before the master leaves on a trip, he calls his servants to himself and gives them each a considerable amount of money to care for in his absence. Two of them handle it well and are rewarded, but the third hides his money away. So many of our students have talents and gifts that the Lord has bestowed upon them, but they never use them to His glory. We need to train and encourage these student leaders to use their gifts in the here and now.

Vision Check

Last year, I let my youngest daughter drive us to her appointment. At that time, she only had her learner's permit. She was somewhat apprehensive because, up to this point, she had only driven with her mom. She didn't want me to be the passenger; she wanted me to drive because she thought I would be critical of her driving abilities and make her uncomfortable. I told her that she needed to drive and that she was going to do great. As we drove, she became more and more confident, and that confidence put her at ease. First, I had to convince her that she could do it. Second, once we got in the car, it gave me the ability to help train her and to encourage her (I think my fingernail impressions are still visible on the car door handle, but she did great!).

Once we have covered the importance of from where and from whom their gifting comes, we begin the process of helping students develop their ministry plans. There is a questionnaire we give them with simple questions. It is geared to help them grasp a realistic picture of what their responsibilities are and what is expected of them, but more importantly, it is meant to encourage them to think outside the box and dream. Here are the questions:

- What is your ministry?
- In your opinion, what makes this a ministry rather than just a religious activity?
- What is your dream for your ministry?
- How will your ministry be an overall blessing to God?
- Do you have a desire to see your ministry grow? Why or why not?
- If so, how can you grow your ministry?
- Do you think that students will want to be part of your ministry? Why or why not?

Let's take a look at these questions.

What is your ministry?

This is the first question on the questionnaire, and it is designed to be somewhat of a trick question because of the way it's worded. New student leaders will always write down what their ministry focus is, such as service, prayer, video, or drama. But the correct answer is much bigger than that single focus. The correct answer is that *all* Christians are called to serve (1 Peter 4:10; John 12:26; Galatians 5:13). With that said, the challenge is for them to discern whether they have a heart to serve others. They should think, "Do I want to serve simply because I'm now in charge, or have I always wanted to serve?" Not having a consistent desire to serve does not disqualify them; but discerning their motives should serve as a wake-up call. They need to understand that it's more than just an activity with an earthly outcome; it's all done by God through us, for His Kingdom and His glory. It's like pulling back the curtain to reveal something to them that can change their lives. You may be thinking that statement is a little over the top, but I would disagree. For *all* believers, that moment that we fully understand why we do what we do is, indeed, life-changing. Look at Colossians 3:23:

> *Whatever you do, work heartily, as for the Lord and not for men.*

When we work for the Lord, we are Kingdom-focused. Once the discussion on this question is complete, the second question can be more clearly understood and answered.

In your opinion, what makes this a ministry rather than just a religious activity?

It is imperative to train our student leaders that this is not just an activity-driven gathering or group. They need to know, understand, and buy into the overall purpose of this, which is to serve Christ by obediently serving those around us. We need them to see the difference between religious activity and ministry. Religious activity is, simply put, people trying to please God by their own works and merits. Ministry is an offshoot of a personal relationship with Jesus Christ. It manifests itself through the believer who is being obedient to the commands of scriptures. So to put it in lay terms, one is trying, and the other is trusting.

What is your dream for your ministry?

After the first two questions are handled, the student leader being interviewed can cast his or her vision for the team. This is always an enjoyable moment for me. I get to hear what they dream of doing. Some students are a little apprehensive, but others dream really, really big. This is where you as the youth minister need to change hats at least a couple of times. You will be one who influences, encourages, or wrangles. You must influence your apprehensive students to think outside the box and dream. You must encourage the students who have a clear vision, and wrangle in the students who dream of ending world hunger in a week.

On both ends of the spectrum, you need to move carefully. Don't scare away your apprehensive students, and don't discourage your big dreamers. Be real and honest with them. I had to learn not to lead the way I want it to go. I have to remind myself not to be a spin doctor. The Merriam Webster online dictionary defines a spin doctor as "a person . . . whose job involves trying to control the way something . . . is described to the public in order to influence what people think about it."[3]

Sometimes we try to help student leaders manage their ministries, or at times we even create something new within their ministries. That is definitely a mistake. There is no

---

3. *Merriam Webster Dictionary*, accessed June 3, 2017, https://www. merriam-webster.com/dictionary/spin%20doctor.

doubt that adults can be creative, imaginative, and great at administration, but we must focus on enabling our student leaders to lead and not inadvertently making them follow us.

I had a student who was leading one of our ministry teams and doing a great job. The ministry was active, vibrant, and seemingly successful. At one of our monthly meetings, the student leader was not enthusiastic at all, which was out of character for her. I pulled her aside at the next Wednesday night service and asked her about the ministry and her thoughts about how it was going. She said she was probably going to step aside and let someone else lead it. I was shocked. I prodded her about what was making her want to step away from her ministry that was doing so well. She finally told me that her Ministry Coach was not allowing her to start some new things she wanted to do. She said the things the ministry was currently involved in were her ideas, but her Ministry Coach had changed how she wanted to do them. I asked her not to step down from her position and to let me help her get back behind the steering wheel. I talked with her Ministry Coach about the situation. She told me that she did give a lot of advice but was unaware that it had frustrated the student. She admitted that she had put her spin on things because she thought it would be better for the ministry. After our meeting, she met with her student leader, apologized, and has since been the model Ministry Coach.

The ministry took on an entirely different look and did not miss a beat in its effectiveness for our Savior. The student's attitude was different. She was enthusiastic and constantly coming up with new ideas for her ministry team. We as adults need to remember that there will be times when some instruction is needed, but we must fight the desire to do too much. Spin is a great thing; just let it be the student's spin. Now this process takes a little time, so don't rush it. And by all means, enjoy it as you watch the students dream. You are seeing them blossom into the leaders that God desires them to be.

How will your ministry be an overall blessing to God?

The center of this ministry focus is not just moralistic activities to benefit humankind. To help student leaders be able to answer this question correctly, it is very important that we always keep the big picture in front of them. Teach them that the purpose of any activity is always for the glory of Christ. They are not promoting a church, people group, or themselves. They are glorifying God through their actions. Through these actions, people can become drawn to Him and hopefully come to know Him in a personal and intimate manner. That should be the desire of each ministry team. I like to ask them, "Do you want to spread the truth of the gospel? Then simply live the gospel. Live it unapologetically before others as you love them and serve them on a daily basis."

Do you have a desire to see your ministry grow? Why or why not?

Student leaders need to have a desire to see growth within their ministries—more hands, more ministry. We just have to make sure their desire to see it happen is for the right reason. Unfortunately, there are a lot of people I know who view desired growth in churches as some sort of stigma, that if you pursue growth, you are being unspiritual. I had gotten used to that mindset, but then I attended a youth workers' conference several years ago, and the breakout session I went to talked about this very issue. The speaker was a professor from a nearby seminary. He explained that the New Testament discusses numerical growth (Acts 2:41, 47; 1 Corinthians 3:7–8). It should be a focus, but a focus for the glory of God and not for people. Student leaders need to understand the *why* of this question so they will be on guard for two things: pride and laziness. Both are deadly!

If so, how can you grow your ministry?

I have yet to have a new student leader who actually had an answer to this question. They generally have some ideas but nothing thought out or planned. As student leaders build relationships with other students, this will typically be a building mechanism for their ministries. But they cannot just rely on that approach (we will talk a little more about relationships in the next question). Once they get their ministry rolling, their Ministry Coach can help them formulate a plan to help them recruit additional team members. Some of the ideas over the years have been really creative.

Do you think that students will want to be part of your ministry? Why or why not?

Teaching our student leaders to be an undershepherd is a major first step in their training. An undershepherd is a lower-ranking shepherd who works under another shepherd (that other shepherd they are working under is you, but ultimately it is the Lord). We want them to be a shepherd to their team, not just a project planner. Sheep trust the shepherd, follow the shepherd, and even come when the shepherd calls. A shepherd knows his sheep, and the sheep know the shepherd. This trust-centered relationship is produced because of time spent together. I have tried to encourage my leaders to spend time with their team, but in a lot of cases, schedules get in the way (students are busier than they have ever been—amen?).

The goal is to build the relationship through communication. It is very important that student leaders be taught the value of communication. To reiterate what was mentioned earlier, communication is paramount in building strong, healthy relationships. We encourage our leaders to contact their team members at least twice a month. This is done through phone calls, texts, e-mails, social media, and personally visiting before and after church services and activities. To team members, being contacted by their leaders means they matter. Knowing they matter helps students feel more confident and builds their confidence in the leader. The leader, because of the continuing contact, gets to know his or her team and develops a heartfelt concern for the students.

A cool thing happens when good communication is established. You see a ministry team become a family. The leaders care for their team members, the team members have confidence in their leader, and the leaders are no longer herding but rather directing. Relationships are imperative, and they make communication, once again, paramount.

If you are part of something special, you want others to experience it as well (pyramid schemes are a great and somewhat irritating example). You invite friends to things that you are excited about, and growth takes place. Growth is a good thing, but of course, it should never be the focus of the team. Remember, obedience to our calling as Christians is first and foremost, but people tend to flock to something that is alive, vibrant, and real. When a student is properly leading his or her ministry team, an amazing thing takes place: the team naturally grows numerically. We never want our student leaders to build their teams to include just their close friends (clique) or just a few easy-to-lead students (minions). We want them to build a team that can accomplish every task they put in front of them. You need to instill in your student leaders a desire to minister to their team members and also see their team grow. The purpose of growth, as stated before, is to accomplish even more ministry.

All Cars, Please Report to the Starting Line

Now that your "drivers" have been selected and their instruction has begun, it's time to get the car ready to go. The next step is to build the rest of the team.

Chapter 6

GET THEM IN THE CAR (OVERALL STUDENT RECRUITMENT)

A few years ago, at a national youth ministers' conference, I attended a session led by Dr. Chap Clark. He made the statement that this is the most untrusting generation we have ever seen. It's this distrust that shows us again why communication is so important.

As I have said before, I am a skeptic by nature. When I read an article or a quote on the Internet, especially on social media, I almost always question its validity. If it is published by a source I know and trust, I usually accept it. I often see this in our students and their parents within the student ministry setting. Students with whom I have built a relationship will trust what I say (unless it involves the words *smell this,* but that's a different story). Those students who do not have an ongoing relationship with me are typically skeptical by nature. Skepticism is a protective device that pretty much all of us seem to have to a certain degree today. We ask questions: "Why should I take your word for it?" "Is what you are saying really true?" "What do you gain from this?" "What does this cost me?" "Why should I trust you?" Those are just a small sample of questions I have encountered over the years. So to be more successful in the recruitment phase (and our ministries as a whole), we have to make sure we have diligently constructed a bridge of trust; this is done through time spent building relationships and most definitely keeping our word.

Here is a question I want to stop and ask at this point: How are you building and maintaining relationships within your ministry? When I was finishing up my undergrad degree, I had to write a thesis, which I titled, "Effective Youth Ministry in a Postmodern Culture." My number-one finding in my research was that if I was going to be effective in youth ministry, then relationship was the key factor.

Please understand that I am not diminishing the proper place of God's power; it is always primary. I am just pointing out that from the human involvement perspective, relationships are key. Because the trust factor is so fragile, and even non-existent at times, we have to work hard to establish and nurture relationships in order to have the opportunity to be invited into a student's world. This takes time, so before you begin to initialize any program or ministry within your sphere of influence, make sure your students (and adults) know you well enough to trust you. Have you invested time and energy building a viable and healthy relationship with those in your ministry spectrum? Also, are you encouraging your student leaders and Ministry Coaches to foster and nurture relationships as well?

Just to clarify, the next section of this chapter is focused on recruiting other students to join these youth-led ministry teams. The area of recruitment encompasses much more than that singular focus. We want to see our ministries grow, and recruitment is not the term we want to use or say to convey what we want to see take place in our ministries. We, as youth ministers, do not desire to recruit students just for the sake of religious activity. We want to see students drawn to a life-changing opportunity to minister and serve that will continue to grow them throughout their spiritual journeys.

As you read this chapter, there will be principles that will apply not only to bringing students in for the sake of ministry service, but also bringing them into the ministry as a whole.

Two Levels of Recruitment

On many occasions, we as youth ministers think that recruitment lies solely on our shoulders. In this ministry model, it does not. Let's be realistic. In many cases, depending on the size of a group, we cannot have a close relationship with every student who attends our ministry activities. Also, most of us cannot roam freely on the junior high and high school campuses with the goal of working on relationships. However, our students have many more opportunities to build relationships on their campuses, during extracurricular activities, and on their jobs than we ever will. That is why we recognize two levels or two avenues of recruitment. One level falls on our shoulders as the youth minster, and the other falls on our students.

Students on the Recruitment Trail

The responsibility of students to recruit students is shared by all the students, not just the student leaders. Once we had a student who was involved with our video ministry team. He was not the leader, but he was a great recruiter for that team. We had a lot of students who became part of making videos because he invited them, and through that invitation, our ministry was able to build relationships with them and see them attend other activities.

Students already have a built-in advantage that we do not have: they are peers, which puts them in a position of acceptance and trust (in most cases).

When new students come into our youth ministry, our focus in this ministry model is to get them involved in a ministry team if we can. I encourage them, but as I stated before, I never force them to join. It's important to remember that there will always be some students who will not become part of an ongoing ministry team. I used to think that if students didn't get involved, I was failing somehow. Then I realized that it's my responsibility to make opportunities available (not just regarding ministry teams, but ministry in general); the act of pursuing service opportunities was on them. That was such a freeing moment for me. So now, when any type of recruitment is going on, I make sure that it is always in a very low-pressure setting. At our monthly meetings with student leaders, I always ask if they have been contacting their team members as well as recruiting new members to serve with them. It's important to always keep them aware of recruitment.

Once a year we host a ministry fair. We do this at the end of August every year, which coincides with the beginning of the school year. We usually bring in pizza, have door prizes, and try to make it a fun time for everyone. We start with music and then have a Bible study that focuses on service. At the end of that time, the student leaders come on the stage, introduce themselves, and talk briefly about their teams and what they do. After that is done, we start the fair. Each ministry team is given a table to set up for their ministry. They decorate them, put out candy or cookies, and then stand by their tables to talk to students about the opportunities their ministries offer. It is so much fun to walk around and listen to the students talk to other students about their ministries. You can hear the excitement and pride coming out; they want everyone to join them. There is a sign-up list at each table, and we instruct the students to sign up for no more than two ministry teams. On a side note, signing up for a particular ministry does not mean that the student cannot help out with other ministries if they have a need. You just don't want the student spread too thin. Once that fair is over, a copy of the sign-up list is given to the leaders to begin contacting their new team members.

One area of caution that I explain to the leaders is to not feel rejected or take it personally when students do not sign up with them. For example, our discipleship team is usually our smallest squad. As you will see in the next chapter, this ministry is comprised of mainly juniors and seniors. Because of the level of commitment and also the age requirement, there are fewer students who sign up for it. The leader needs to understand that this is just going to happen and to not be disappointed. There will also be times that a ministry may not have anyone sign up. That has been our drama ministry for the last couple of years. I have allowed past leaders who really had a burden to lead it to do monologues or work with the video team in writing scripts. But it is important to help your leaders develop realistic expectations. I tell them to picture their recruitment time at the fair as a blank canvas and just wait to see what God paints. I encourage them to spend time in prayer that God will bring to them the right team members and to also do everything they can to help others catch their vision.

Adults on the Recruiting Trail

As for our place as adults in the recruitment process, we need to always be encouraging students to be involved. We have to remember the benefits of this ministry model and why students need to be involved. We see more and more students today who just want to sit back and do very little. This can be frustrating, especially when you see their potential and giftedness. Encouragement is key, but do not push. I speak from experience when I say that if you push too hard, the student may leave the ministry. A lot of these students who sit back and never commit will show up to help teams who need it. Last year, our youth deacons and young ladies ministry team joined together to help a family move. There in the midst of this work project were four students who refused to sign up for any ministry team, but they were there, and they worked hard. I have seen them at other work projects as well. What I found out was that they just did not want to be committed. They believed that if they signed up for a ministry team, they would be required to be there for everything. I tried to explain to them that such was not the case, but they still chose to be uncommitted. Just like the students, adults also need to understand that rejection is not personal, and it should not discourage them.

We also need to be very aware of and cautious of blind trust. What I mean by blind trust is that there will be times that a student who does not know us that well will trust us. Because of the position in which we serve, there will be students who are conditioned to trust us because of our authority. They may think that because we're their youth ministers or ministry leaders/volunteers, they can trust us. All it takes is one misstep on our part, and the trust is crushed.

Years ago, there was an eighth-grade boy who lived near our family. His younger brother played with my son Christopher. I didn't know him that well, but he was a very confident young man who was very accomplished in the martial arts. I had spoken with him at times, but it was always brief. One night I hosted a lock-in at the church, and I was able to talk him into coming. Later in the evening, we played a game—really it was more of a prank, involving a quarter, a blindfold, a funnel, and a pitcher of ice water (some of you see where this is going). He volunteered, and I readily called him up to participate in the game. I assumed that he was secure enough to play the game. But once the prank hit its mark, he stood there with ice-cold wet blue jeans while the other students laughed. He pulled off the blindfold, looked down at his jeans, looked at the crowd, and ran down the hallway and out into the parking lot. I was right behind him, apologizing and asking him to stop and talk to me. Once we were in the parking lot, he stopped, turned around with tears in his eyes, and screamed, "Why? Why would you do this to me? I *trusted* you!" With that, he turned and ran home. Eventually, he and I made amends for that night, but he never came back to the church. That is a pretty drastic story, but I want to drive home the point of being cautious with the trust students have in us. If we violate our students' trust, we take the chance that we will never get the opportunity to help train them in their spiritual journey.

Keeping It Clear

Working diligently to keep the stage clear of skepticism is paramount. As I said at the beginning of this chapter, students today are untrusting, so we must work with our adults and student leaders to ensure that we are doing everything possible to guard the trust that is placed in us by those who are following us. If there is even the smallest amount of skepticism, students will usually not go forward. So within this ministry model, two things need to be guarded. Communication is the first one. It is key in this process. Unspoken or poorly communicated expectations can bring a lot of frustration and heartache. Both students and adults need to ensure that communication is well done.

The second revolves around integrity. A life without integrity or even a momentary lapse that others see can be very detrimental to what we are trying to establish in our ministries. Look at the words in Titus 2:7-8:

Show yourself in all respects to be a model of good works, and in your teaching show integrity, dignity, and sound speech that cannot be condemned, so that an opponent may be put to shame, having nothing evil to say about us.

These verses say that if we are without integrity, people will have a negative view of us. This affects more than just us. We cannot lose sight that we strive for integrity for the glory of the Lord, and that a lack of integrity will destroy trust in relationships . . . quickly. As leaders, we must understand that we are to work our hardest to keep our word, no matter how insignificant we may think that word is. An unkept promise can bring distrust into a relationship in a heartbeat.

The Clown Car

I remember as a kid that I was mesmerized by a particular moment at the circus. It was that moment when all the clowns would pile into a very small car. Clowns just kept coming and coming, and they kept jumping into that tiny car. There always seemed to be room for one more. To me, they didn't run out of room; they ran out of clowns. In this ministry model, there is always room for one more. Therefore, recruiting never stops. When new students find their way to your ministry, there should always be room for one more in any of your ministries. Encourage your student leaders and your adults to be looking to grow. I have seen ministries in the past that just got comfortable. Their teams became self-centered social cliques that created programmed events rather than Christ-centered ministries. In those cases, the ministry members became discouraged and disgruntled. Make sure that complacency does not settle in and that the leaders are striving to get one more into the car.

Chapter 7

MINISTRY TEAMS

Determining what ministry teams you will be able to offer is based on your students and their desires. Getting to this phase is always exciting because we are getting close to turning the students loose. In this chapter, I want to give you some examples of ministry teams that our youth ministry utilizes.

Service Teams

Service teams are simply what the title says. It is a team (or teams) focused on serving each other, the church, and the community. In our youth ministry, we divided this team into two: youth deacons and the young ladies ministry team (although these teams are separate, they quite often overlap). They're responsible for finding service opportunities. Here are some of the service projects that these teams have accomplished:

- Yard and housework for widows, single moms, and people in need
- Nursing home visits
- Making meals for families in need
- Helping families move from one home to the next
- Community volunteering (the YMCA, Boys & Girls Clubs)
- Serving at our local shelter (led by our missions team)
- Volunteering at our local Pregnancy Care Center
- Working around the church
- Serving during church activities or services

The list could be even longer. You'll be amazed at how many opportunities will present themselves once your team is established.

Typically, as the youth minister, people will approach you with a need or present a need to you. In that case, I simply relay it to the student leaders and let them run with it. Another fun aspect of this ministry is that you can just go along on a service project and simply be a worker and watch your students lead.

Prayer Team

The prayer team is what I would call a priority ministry because it is greatly needed within the student ministry. It teaches students to bring their requests to our Heavenly Father and rely on Him. When done properly, a student-led prayer ministry team takes the focus off the students' abilities and puts it on the Lord's abilities.

We have several methods available to get prayer requests to our team. There are prayer cards and an iPad kiosk in the back of our student center where students can relay their prayer needs. On our website, we have a link where students can submit a prayer request and a QR code they can scan with their mobile devices to submit requests that way. Our prayer team meets every week in our student center 45 minutes before our service to pray. They pray over the requests they have received and also for that night's service.

At the end of our Bible study time on Wednesday nights, we sometimes close our service with one last song. At that time, a few students from the prayer team (and other ministry teams as well) come to the front of the stage and face the other students so students can come forward and be prayed for by these team members. Again, it's so cool to see students ministering to their peers.

Periodically, it's a good idea to have your prayer team share during a service or event what the Lord has done through answered prayer. This gives an automatic reminder to those present that God is listening and prayer is there for them. The most remarkable point is that they are hearing from their peers that prayer works.

Connect Team

The connect team used to be known as the greeters' ministry, but that title seemed to give an incorrect definition of what the team is all about. It's not just about greeting people; it's about connecting with them. The connect team works to make sure that visitors and also regulars are greeted and made to feel welcome at any event we host. The team also mails a postcard to visitors, letting them know they were glad to have met them and hope to see them again. Another responsibility this team has is to send birthday greetings, get well wishes, notes of congratulations, and thank you notes. This is done through snail mail, texting, e-mail, Facebook, Instagram, and any other social media the students are using.

I talked earlier about a thesis I had to write on ministry in a postmodern culture. I shared how building relationships is key. Building connections is also an important part of ministry today. When our students are the ones doing it, more doors are open to them than to us. The connect team is a powerful tool to open doors.

Discipleship/Mentor Team

I love seeing students take part in other students' lives for the betterment of their Christian journey. This is especially true when it comes to students discipling students. When this takes place, the ones discipling truly take on the role of a shepherd. Shepherds want to see their flocks grow in the faith; as this is happening, the ones leading the discipling grow as well.

We use a simple 13-week curriculum that invites students to study essential biblical aspects of their faith such as prayer, service, salvation, and so on. This study causes the students to look up a variety of scriptures as they relate to the subject of that chapter. There are also weekly Bible verses they have to memorize. Once they have completed that study and would like to continue, we have a second one for them that is a little more involved.

The students who are involved with this ministry team are some of your most committed students. The commitment is a huge undertaking for a student. Once a week for 13 weeks (or more if they go on to the next study), they meet with the one whom they are discipling. We encourage the leader to be punctual and prepared. This is a ministry team that you do not want to launch until you have found, screened, and trained the right students for the responsibility. Nothing will squash a student's enthusiasm faster than to see in another student's eyes that they are not worth their time. Do not rush into this. Take your time and do it right.

This team is mainly juniors and seniors. There have been certain situations in which we have allowed younger students to lead, but they have always discipled a younger student. An active Ministry Coach is a must for this ministry.

Missions Team

I love missions! Opportunities are everywhere. You don't have to climb into an airplane and jet off to a foreign destination to do missions (even though those kinds of missions are always amazing). The missions team helps the ministry identify possible missions work, whether it's a hands-on project or a fund-raising event for another missions organization. The leader is taught to filter each opportunity and examine it as closely as possible. The leader might ask, "What are their needs?" "How can we partner with them?" "What kind of commitment will be required of us?" "Are we actually capable of meeting their needs?" They are also challenged to try to get the most bang out of a buck—in other words, they need to practice good stewardship. We take up a monthly offering on Wednesday nights for a mission need that the missions team has decided to adopt for that quarter. The team looks for missions opportunities on three levels: local, national, and international.

Our definition of local missions work is projects that take place within an hour's radius of our church. They are opportunities such as running elementary school Bible clubs, volunteering at our local mission, working at our summer children's carnival outreach, and any other local ministry opportunity that presents itself. For these events, they work hand-in-hand with our service team ministries.

National missions are mission projects that are more than an hour from our church and within the continental United States. That is usually our summer missions trip that we take each year. The missions team helps in the preliminary planning of this trip.

International missions are a big deal, and we do not have a large group that goes every year. It is usually small groups. For an international missions trip, the missions team helps the ones taking the trip to raise funds and set up prayer support with our prayer team.

Worship Team

Nearly every youth ministry has students with a desire to do something with music. It could be a choir, an ensemble, or a worship team. I have had numerous students over the years go into vocational ministry, but most of them have gone into music ministry. Your Ministry Coach will have to put a lot of time into this ministry simply because of the need to practice, practice, practice. On occasion, your Ministry Coach may be a musician. Be sure to remind these Ministry Coaches that they are not to build a band around themselves, but to stand on the outside and help where necessary. I mentioned earlier in the book that I have a high expectation level when it comes to youth ministry and I have a hard time delegating because of that. This ministry team has really helped me become better at that. Let's face it, it's sometimes difficult to endure the first time a new worship team leads a service because of their inexperience. But what makes it actually enjoyable is seeing their excitement for their new ministry. Given time, this ministry only gets better and will become, in my experience, one of the ministry's biggest draws for other students to attend your services.

Wednesday Night Ministry Team

We host a mid-week service on Wednesday night each week for an hour and 45 minutes. We have music and a Bible study—those are anchor items—but we try to keep things fresh by doing a variety of other things from week to week. Videos, dramas, small mixer games, outdoor games, student testimonies, ministry updates, missions offerings, and giveaways are all items we rotate in and out from week to week. Making sure the program runs well falls on the Wednesday night ministry team. It is their responsibility to make sure everything is in place and goes according to schedule. They check with the worship team, that night's speaker, the audiovisual team, and any others who are in charge of any element scheduled for that night's service to ensure that everything is in place. Bottled water, podiums, chairs, extra batteries, and such are a few of the items they make sure are on hand and ready, if needed. They also make sure the video countdown starts on time, that the personalities for that night have assembled for prayer at the appointed time, and that any latecomers have found a seat. Throughout the service, the team is constantly keeping an eye out for the needs of the evening. Because of the demands they have to shoulder, it is good for them to be on a rotating schedule. That's to make sure they are being spiritually fed as well.

One aspect of this team that I love is hearing their feedback and letting them make suggestions for the upcoming services. When this occurs, it adds a different dynamic to the team. It is no longer just about serving by meeting the needs of that night's service, but it allows them to have a vested interest in the planning as well.

Now you may be thinking that your service doesn't need this kind of team because of the number that attend your youth ministry, but note that ours is not a huge youth group. Maybe orchestrating the evening event does not need to occur, but allowing your students to have a say in your weekly meeting does, in my opinion. Instead of your students just showing up for an event that has been planned for them, they are showing up because they have a vested interest in what's going on, and this brews—wait for it—enthusiasm!

Video and Photography Team

The video and photography team is by far the most popular of all of our ministry teams. Why is it so popular? Think about this: when we look at group pictures, who is it that we look for first? Yep, you guessed it—ourselves. Students love to see themselves in the videos. They love to see their friends in videos as well. This is a great ministry that lets them turn their creative juices loose and have some fun.

I ask them to create videos to advertise an upcoming event or a Bible study illustration. But their favorite video endeavor is making rules videos for overnight events. Many of them are outright hilarious! There are moments that are cringe-worthy, but most of the time it's so cringe-worthy that it's funny.

Always make guidelines for them to abide by, and for the love of all that is right, review *every* video before you show it. I know that is a *duh* statement, but it only takes one moment of an unreviewed video to find yourself suddenly updating your résumé (boy, do I have a few stories). This not only applies to videos but also to taking pictures at events.

Arts Ministry Team (Drama, Painting, Puppets, Etc.)

The arts have a tremendous impact on people. A simple monologue, a heartfelt drama presentation, or even a painted picture can be used by God to bring about eternal change in a person's life. In a world that has become more entertainment and media driven, the church must find new methods to deliver the unchanging message of hope and salvation through Jesus Christ to a constantly changing world. That is where the arts ministry comes into play. It's another ministry that requires a dedicated Ministry Coach because of the practice that is required.

Audiovisual Media Team

The audiovisual media team's focus is to make sure the media and audio needs are met at all of our youth events.

On Wednesday nights, the team works with the band, the video team, the drama team (if they are performing), and the speaker for that night to make sure that all the audiovisual needs for the evening service are taken care of. Although the Wednesday night youth services are our main need for this ministry, there are a lot of other needs. They also work with other teams to meet their ministry needs. For example, if the recreation team plans to do outdoor games, the audiovisual team makes sure that any audio needs are taken care of. If the outreach team plans an event, they work with the audiovisual team to make sure their needs are meet. We could build a lot of other scenarios, but you can see that there are many areas for this team to be a blessing and an asset.

Recreation Team

For me personally, the recreation team is a lot of fun to watch. We expect to see creativity from certain ministries like the drama, video, and outreach teams, but the recreation team brings an entirely different spin on creativity. When we started the recreation team, I figured we'd use the games we already knew or pull some from resources we had on hand. But that wasn't the case. I saw the leaders dream and plan activities that were so creative and innovative that my thoughts on this ministry became totally different. This team plans recreation for Wednesday nights, discipleship weekends, youth camps, and retreats. They also work with the outreach team to help them carry out their vision if recreation is to be part of the event.

Administration Team

The administration team is a great ministry for your introverted students because this is definitely a behind-the-scenes ministry. The student leaders who head up this ministry need to be more mature due to the nature of the information they handle. They can handle event registrations, keeping up with year-round medical release forms, and any online and physical paperwork that needs to be done. Also, on the day of an event, they can handle the check-in table, instructing people where they need to go, and numerous other responsibilities.

Outreach Team

The outreach team is a great ministry for gaining insight into a student's world. We as youth ministers plan events and programs that we think will be of interest to students in hopes of drawing them in. Let's be honest, I haven't always been on point in events I have planned in hopes of drawing in students. Having a student-led outreach team gives you access to their world. They know what is trending, what their peers are drawn to, and what to avoid. Having a team like this in place can give your ministry an edge. Granted, some of their ideas (if actually implemented) could cause you to update your résumé (just like the video team), but that doesn't happen very often. As I said before, don't limit their dreams.

Start by Giving Them Ownership

I know I haven't covered all that's out there when it comes to ministry opportunities for our students. I encourage you, if you plan on using this model, to allow your students ownership in the vision of the ministry. They sometimes see things we don't see. It could be a ministry that needs to be started, one that needs to combined with another, or one that does not need to be started at that time. If you give them ownership right at the starting block, you can see excitement build.

There will be times you may want your student leaders to just be students. Make sure that you give your leaders, as well as their team, a chance to not have to think about service responsibilities. There will be times when we plan certain events that could use the help of a certain student-led ministry, but we will ask them to just come and be ministered to instead of leading.

Chapter 8

HANDING OVER THE KEYS

Implementing

Now it's time to let our students drive! It's what they have been waiting for since you began this new ministry direction. Here is where your patience will grow—and it has to. One thing to remember is that as they begin their ministries, at first *encourage* them to take baby steps, but don't *force* them to. The last thing you want them to experience is an immediate struggle right out of the box, although some of life's greatest teachable moments come from struggles. Think of the butterfly coming out of its cocoon. It has to struggle to get out, but by God's design there is a purpose for that struggle. If there weren't a struggle, then the butterfly's wings would not be strong enough to fly. Struggles or difficulties are not to be feared. If they happen, it's our job to encourage students through it. Of course, there will be times when their dreams are, by our earthly perspective, just too big, but let them dream. Until now, you have been riding shotgun, giving instructions and making sure they understand what is necessary to make this ministry go. Now you have to get out of the way and watch them take it around the block on their own. You have now entered into a new era of ministry, a place where you are no longer just a minister *to* but also a minister *with* students.

Jesus Is the Greatest Teacher

Jesus gives us an example, an incredible illustration of what it is like to turn others out to minister. Let's take a look at that in Luke 9–10. At the end of Luke 9, we find Jesus and His disciples heading to Jerusalem. Along their journey, they come to a Samaritan village, which turns them away. Jesus's disciples, namely John and James, want to call down judgment to destroy the village because of this rejection. Jesus rebukes them and reminds them that He did not come to destroy, but to save. As they continue on their journey, three men interact with Jesus about being His disciples (followers). With each one, He reminds them that to be a true disciple, they must make a radical commitment.

Let's look at Luke 10:1:

After this the Lord appointed seventy-two others and sent them on ahead of him, two by two, into every town and place where he was about to go.

The verse begins with the word *after*. That's significant because it shows the close time proximity to the events that just took place, the rejection in the village, and the call to radical commitment. Those two events set the stage for what Jesus was about to do, which was to send them out. He wanted them to be prepared for what they were going to encounter—rejection and personal cost—as they obeyed His instructions. You will soon be in that situation as well. You will train your students, and then it will be time to let them lead their ministries. This is what the chapter is all about. One more important thing this passage reveals is how the disciples return. Luke 10:17 tells us something encouraging:

The seventy-two returned with joy (emphasis added).

This is something I have seen over and over again in student ministry. When students are released to go and fulfill the responsibilities of their ministry teams, there is usually a great excitement in them. I love this passage in the Bible because it reinforces the importance of preparation and the significance of release. It reminds me of the moments when my kids rode their bicycles for the first time without training wheels and the big smile they had that expressed their joy. Hearing each of them say, "Look Mom, look Dad! I'm doing it!" as they pedaled furiously down the street. I won't forget the joy my wife and I felt as well as we enjoyed their success. Now, as a parent of several children with driver's licenses, I can remember those pride-filled moments when they walked out of the department of motor vehicles holding their new driver's licenses. It's that moment you realize that they have been taught, tested, and proved and can now legally drive a car. As a youth minister or youth worker, you have now reached that point with your students. You have instructed and prepared them, and now it is time for them to be allowed to take the ministry on their own. It is time to hand over the keys and release them to take ownership.

Two Ways to Launch

By this time, you have decided you will look at your group and choose how many ministry teams you're going to have. Now you have to determine how quickly you want to turn them loose to lead their own ministry teams. It's either a slow-off-the-line or pedal-to-the-metal approach. Let me explain the two.

Slow off the Line

This approach is simply creating and releasing one ministry at a time. When we first started using this ministry approach, that's how we did it. It's a really good approach to take when you are first starting. Keep in mind that not only do you need time to train your student leaders, but you also need time to train your adults. It truly is easier on the youth minister. When you have a slower approach to creating and releasing your ministry teams, you are not as dependent on your volunteers. It gives your adults a chance to learn at a slower pace. I have learned that they and the student leaders can get overwhelmed and frustrated if they do not fully understand every part of their responsibilities. I've had Ministry Coaches quit because they were overwhelmed by simply not fully understanding what was required of them. So a slow start is not a bad thing, especially if this is a new approach for your ministry.

Pedal to the Metal

I have also helped youth ministries launch their ministry teams with the pedal-to-the-metal approach. Where I am now in my ministry, I love this approach. It has a lot of excitement that goes along with it. It's like drinking your favorite beverage from a fire hydrant! If you are up to the challenge and are committed to properly training all the leaders leading up to the launch date, then this approach is for you. What I suggest to churches that want to start this way is to plan a special day when all your teams will launch together.

First, coordinate with all your leaders to simultaneously do a ministry project or training with their teams on that day. It might be service projects, video shooting, audiovisual training, a prayer gathering, discipleship orientation, drama or worship team practice, and so on. Having a specific kickoff day brings an excitement to the table and accountability for your leaders (this is especially needed with your newbies) to get off the starting block. Remember what it was like the night before a big day? Maybe it was the night before your high school graduation, the night before you left for college, the night before your wedding day, or whatever special moment you can think of at this moment. Sleep did not come easily that night because of the anticipation. That's something our students have shared with me. Set a date when the keys are officially handed over. This date, if handled and promoted correctly, will be greatly anticipated. It's a date that our students (again, especially our newbies) look forward to each year. It is that moment when they finally feel like the ministry is theirs to run. At one of your monthly meetings, set a date for the kickoff. Make sure you give them plenty of time to plan, advertise, and recruit for that day's activities. On that day, make sure your adult encouragers are on hand as well. For our student ministry, the kickoff day looks like this:

9:15 a.m. – Meet with the student ministry team leaders (usually over coffee, juice, and donuts).

10:00 a.m. – Meet at your designated location with your team.

1:00 p.m. – Meet at the church for lunch and talkback.

2:00 p.m. – Dismiss.

The hopeful outcome of this day is for a wave of excitement to overtake your youth ministry. Now comes the fun part—watching them drive!

Chapter 9

KEEPING THE CAR MOVING

Now that you have successfully released the teams to go and fulfill their vision for their ministries, your work is done, right? Umm, that would be a negative! You've worked alongside your students to pick a car, you've trained the coaches (we'll call them the pit crew for a moment), trained the drivers, put them on the track, and given them the keys. Now you put on a new hat: pit chief. In the course of all this training and preparation, you now have to keep this car moving. I teach my students to understand that this "car" they're now driving has no brakes and they are driving uphill. If they are not moving forward they are rolling backward. It's kind of a scary picture, but it's an accurate one. This is how I view the Christian life. If we are not moving forward, we are going backward. Let's look at some tips for keeping things rolling forward.

Keep Them on the Track

The dream situation is to see all the teams running like clockwork on their own all year long. Let's be real for a moment; they don't always. Our students are easily distracted and also very busy, especially in their senior year. So it's a good idea to have a date on the calendar during the year for all our teams to get together and have strategic planning days. For us, those days are very similar to our kickoff date. By planning these dates a couple of times a year, we give the ministry team leaders a day to come and be encouraged. It's also a great time to build and strengthen their relationships within their teams. These planning dates should not take the place of scheduling their own events. These events work really well to remind them of the ministry's focus or to regain momentum if it has been lost. Keep in mind that encouraging and helping your student leaders to keep the correct focus can also take place at your monthly meetings, but we'll talk about that in just a moment.

These work days can give your student leaders a jump start and a jolt of excitement. Sometimes, we all need to change things up a little.

Encourage Your Pit Crew

Another group that needs encouragement is your Ministry Coaches. There needs to be a lot of consistent communication with these volunteers. They can get frustrated. Youth ministry teams that do not have adequate adult encouragement can often suffer a loss of purpose, drive, and focus. Take a break with your Ministry Coaches and have a special time of encouragement. Plan an event for them and their spouses.

This can be a dinner or a fun activity for them to attend or possibly a day of fun. Whatever you plan, it's a great time for you to strengthen relationships within your adult team and give them some much needed encouragement while having fun together. You do need scheduled times for the Ministry Coaches to come together for accountability and reinforcement in their training. It's a great time to remind them of the difference between encouraging and taking control of a ministry team. There are times that I don't have any issue with a coach stepping in and leading. But those times should be limited. Ministry Coaches should always be ready to step back. If it becomes a struggle for the student leader when a Ministry Coach steps in, you will usually hear from that student leader. At the same time, be sure students understand what a great benefit it is to have Ministry Coaches who are always there as ready resources to assist them.

Monthly Meetings with the Student Leaders

I love our monthly meetings with student leaders! These meetings are very important to keep the communication lines flowing and relationships strong. A typical meeting starts with dinner and then moves to our living room to talk. I start by asking every ministry leader to give an update on what's going on in their ministry and if there are any needs that we as a ministry can help them with. I also like to get their feedback on the youth activities and programs. I would love to tell you that the meetings run like a well-oiled machine, but let's be real, that's not real life. We chase a lot of rabbits, and we might even catch one every now and again, but the focus of the meeting is accountability through relationships. There is a lot of serious conversation, but there are a lot of stories and laughing, too.

Real Life

If you have been a youth minister for a while, you know good and well that you will have some frustrations. If you're new to the world of youth ministry, just know that it will come. It's just part of what we encounter. I had a pastor friend of mine tell me one time, "It's a fallible world with fallible people, so expect fallible things to happen." Trust me, I'm not being a Negative Ned or a Bitter Bob. I'm just being truthful and real.

When frustration comes, evaluate it. What is the cause? Is it from unfair or unrealistic expectations that you've set? Also, make sure you clearly verbalize your expectations. An unspoken expectation can easily fall into the unfair expectation category pretty quickly. Unfair, unrealistic, and unspoken expectations will only bring frustration for you and the students, so guard yourself from them at all costs. Here are some of the expectations you need to avoid:

- Expecting the student leaders to always be mature and always make good decisions.

- Expecting every student to join a ministry team. We will always have students who show up and do nothing.

- Expecting every student who volunteers to serve on a team to show up at every service opportunity.

- Expecting the student leaders to always stay on top of their responsibilities.
- Expecting things to always run as you would like them to.

Let the students help set the expectations for this ministry model. If your experience is like what I have experienced, you will be amazed at how high most of your students will set the bar. But don't let your fear of frustration keep you from letting your students lead. You'll see so many amazing things that will make your heart almost burst with pride (righteous pride, of course!) as you witness your students be ministers right before your very eyes. And it will be at service projects they have planned, orchestrated, and executed themselves.

You'll encounter three kinds of student leaders: the ones who will work hard, the ones who will not work at all, and the ones who will just quit. In regard to your students who serve well, celebrate them! As for the other two types of leaders, just know that they are out there and that you will encounter them at some point in this ministry model.

When encountering those two kinds of student leaders who do not serve well, you have to realize that you may have to allow ministry teams to remain dormant or scratch them completely. At the moment that I am writing this book, we have 14 ministry teams on the books, but only 10 are actually functioning. If they aren't working, then let them go. You or your Ministry Coaches will have to fight the inclination to do it for the students or just take over in order to make that ministry team continue to function. If it isn't student led, then an adult taking over that ministry defeats the very purpose of why it was created. But make sure that you have a conversation with the student who is the leader of that ministry before you place that ministry on the shelf. Help that leader make the best decision about whether to try to resuscitate the ministry team, let it sit idle for a season, or scratch it completely. That can be a very difficult decision for students to make for many reasons. Help them examine their commitment to the ministry. Do they have enough time for the ministry? Do they have the same passion for the ministry as when they started? I've had to deal with a lot of these situations through the years. Students always feel as if they've failed in some way. In some cases, the ministry died on the vine because of their lack of devotion, but I always want them to stay connected. So it's important to encourage them to get connected to another ministry team. I also want them to know that this does not disqualify them from leading a ministry team in the future. I explain to them that it just wasn't the right time for them to lead. Overall, you need to see what ministry teams work, go after them, and don't let discouragement keep you from giving your students an opportunity to be ministers.

Give Them Something to Look Forward To

The thing our student leaders look forward to all year is an event we call Youth Week. It's a three-day event during the summer that is totally planned by the leaders of these ministry teams. When we meet at the first of the year, I give them a budget amount for the event. Then the fun begins. They have total control of this event. They choose the speaker and the band, create their own artwork, plan all the recreation, decorate the student center and their meeting rooms, and make up all the teams. When it comes to anything about Youth Week, I am just a hired hand—I work for them. I do review all contracts and sign them on behalf of our church, but other than that, I am just their flunky for that event. It's so much fun to see them turned loose and excited. They consider this a special reward for their serving as a leader of a ministry team.

As I said at the beginning of this chapter, you never stop working in this ministry model, but we have to remember why we're doing it—to train students to be lifelong, ministry-minded followers of Christ.

Chapter 10

REMEMBER THE CALL

Why do we read books like this? What are you looking for or hoping to find? If you are like me, you are looking for new ideas or possibly answers to issues you may be experiencing in your youth ministry, or a plethora of other reasons. While I was writing this book, my prayer for it was a simple one: "Father, please use this to further your Kingdom." No book, outside of the Bible, can ever give us the eternal answer to what we need for our ministries, but we can glean from all sorts of sources that will enhance our efforts. I want to finish with four challenges for you. The first one is a simple reminder for all believers, but especially for those of us that are called to serve in youth ministry. Whether you are a full-time or part-time lay leader or volunteer youth worker, we have a singular calling. If we want to see our students stay true to their calling as followers of Christ, then we need to understand the complete picture of what it means to make disciples.

Be Confident

Let's look back at Matthew 28:18–20. Jesus is giving the final instructions to His disciples. He starts in verse 18 by stating that all authority has been given to Him. This is a verse that sometimes will be quickly passed over so the instructions that follow can be the centerpiece of the message. The word for *authority* in the original Greek context is *exousía*, which means official right or power. This power was given to Jesus by the Father. There were two purposes for Jesus to use this word. The first was so the disciples knew that the directive they were about to receive carried a lot of weight and was not just a suggestion; it was a command. This command was from the most ultimate authority that has ever existed, so it was imperative that they be obedient.

One time, two of our children were in a squabble. One was in the bathroom, and the other needed in. The one who needed in was getting nowhere with her pleading and threats, so she approached me to get involved in the situation. I simply told her to go back and tell her sister that Dad said to open the door. Lo and behold, when she recited those words, the door immediately opened. The message had not changed, just the authority behind it. In Matthew 28, Jesus was making sure the disciples understood the authority behind the command so they would fully understand its importance.

The second purpose of this statement was to give the disciples reassurance. By stating that it was God, the creator and sustainer of this world, who was giving them this amazing commission, they were not to be afraid. In Mark 16:18, Mark emphasizes this when he says that God's protection will be over them. Jesus also said in Matthew 28:20 that He would *always* be with them. Wow! What assurance! So they were not to be fearful but rather bold for the sake of the gospel.

I remember one time when the lights in our home went out during the night of a massive storm. My daughter Melissa, who was very young at that time, started calling out for me. I asked her if she was all right, and she answered, "I'm okay now. I just wanted to make sure you were there." In Matthew 28, Jesus was about to leave them to do their tasks. He would not be physically present, and this last statement from Him was to prepare and charge them. By bringing that assurance to the disciples, Jesus instilled in them what was needed for this amazing commission.

As youth ministers, we need to remember the commission and assurance that Jesus spoke to the disciples. As followers of Christ, was are called to live out this verse every day. We should strive to authentically live this out in front of the students with whom we have been entrusted. They should see that confidence and determination in us every single day. When they see us living out our faith like that, they become confident in their own world. Just like my daughter calling out to me that night, our students are looking to see if this faith that we speak about is real to us. If it is, it brings them assurance. I know that because I've been told this numerous times by students and parents alike. Your students are watching you. We have to be careful not to live in a do-as-I-say-not-as-I-do mindset. In other words, don't just preach it, but live it. If we desire to see our students go and fulfill the great commission, we must let our lives be one of the greatest messages ever preached.

Be Guarded

The enemy of God does not want us to be authentic, committed followers, because when we are, we become an amazing representation of God's grace, goodness, and worth. At times, the world can cause us to take our eyes off of the finish line with all sorts of distractions, but please let me encourage you to fight the good fight and never stop. We must guard our hearts! Proverbs 4:23–27 reminds us:

> Keep your heart with all diligence, For out of it spring the issues of life. Put away from you a deceitful mouth, And put perverse lips far from you. Let your eyes look straight ahead, And your eyelids look right before you. Ponder the path of your feet, And let all your ways be established. Do not turn to the right or the left; Remove your foot from evil (NKJV).

This passage is an incredible challenge to us as believers. Take a moment to reflect on every word. The writer is warning us to guard ourselves. Why? Proverbs 3:33 reminds us that God's blessing is on the righteous, not the wicked. God will still use us if we fall away, but not in the way we would desire to be used (2 Timothy 2:20). So be guarded that you might be found faithful in all your pursuits. God has placed an incredible weight of responsibility on the Christian leader's shoulders. We as leaders of our youth ministries must not only faithfully nurture and direct those under our care, but we must also pay careful attention to our personal faith walk. A healthy youth ministry depends on healthy youth ministers whose ministries and personal lives both equally reflect a biblical submission to God. I love Paul's charge to Timothy in 1 Timothy 6:10–11:

> For the love of money is a root of all kinds of evil, for which some have strayed from the faith in their greediness, and pierced themselves through with many sorrows. But you, O man of God, flee these things and pursue righteousness, godliness, faith, love, patience, gentleness (NKJV).

Paul gives Timothy the inspiring call to faithful service and to pursue personal holiness! The six virtues in verse 11 together describe a life that is balanced spiritually. As followers of Christ who are called to lead students into a deeper relationship with Him, we must authentically model these things. You may be thinking, "Aren't these standards impossible for us to attain and keep?" If we think in earthly terms, then yes. But God did not leave us to accomplish this on our own. He has placed in our lives His Holy Spirit, enabling us to be able to live godly lives. Take a moment to reflect on where you are personally. What is the focus of your daily pursuit? Have you let your guard down?

Be Faithful

Look at Matthew 28:19. Here is the directive: make disciples. A proper understanding of this verse will greatly help us in our endeavor to properly prepare and equip our students to not become the next negative statistic in regard to the church.

I get the privilege of meeting people from all over the country. When time permits, I absolutely love the opportunity to sit down with other youth ministers and hear them speak their hearts. I love to hear what God is doing in their worlds, and I love to ask them what works for them in their ministries. It's always a blessing to meet a youth minister who is effectively making disciples. When they share with me what God is doing in their ministries, their faces light up. So what is the proper definition of making disciples? *Make disciples* comes from the Greek verb (imperative mode) *mathēteúō, which* means not only to learn, but to become attached to one's teacher and to become his or her follower in the doctrine and conduct of life.[4]

Occasionally, I meet a youth minister whose prime directive is not to make disciples but to create what I call a moral social club. There is a dabbling in the spiritual, but very little. Colossians 4:5 and Ephesians 5:16 both charge us to redeem the time. We as youth ministers only have a small window to pour as much as we can into the lives of our students. If your focus is not on what it takes to make disciples but only on the social aspects of ministry, then you are not preparing your students for the battles that lie ahead. So if you have been entrusted with a ministry to students, please make sure you are using every opportunity wisely.

---

4. Spiros Zodhiates, *The Complete Word Study Dictionary: New Testament*, 1992.

Be Purposeful

Take a second to answer these questions:

- What is the purpose of my ministry?
- How will I attain this purpose?
- Is this purpose in line with a scriptural model?
- What are the *what* and the *why* of my ministry?

I know that there are numerous books out there that tackle these questions, but I want to touch on this subject for just a brief moment.

As I finish up this last chapter, I'm already researching for my next book, which will cover the *what* and the *why* of youth ministry from my perspective. In preparation for that book, I asked myself these same questions. In fact, through the years, I have asked myself these questions at different times. It is always beneficial to examine what we do to ensure we stay on the right track. Another area of insight is to ask your students to do an evaluation of the ministry. Having their perspective is beneficial and sometimes brutal, but don't shy away from it. We have to make sure that in all we are doing, we are remaining scripturally purposeful. If not, we become the veritable hamster on the wheel—we have a whole lot of activity but we're going nowhere spiritually.

In Matthew 28:20, we are instructed to teach new disciples. But teach them what? "To observe all things" (NKJV), Christ states in that passage. The "all things" refer to the doctrines and commandments of Christ. Simply put, we must teach our students the Word of God. How much biblical teaching on average do you give your students during a week? Are you giving them an opportunity to exercise what they are being taught? Are you doing all the work for them so when they show up they just participate instead of taking a leadership role? Teaching is a lot more than reciting a Bible study. Since you have read through this book, you probably understand that.

Final Thought

I am not an expert on youth ministry by any stretch of the imagination. I have simply tried to tell you what has worked well for me and my ministry. Do I live out my calling perfectly? No. But I do pray every day for God to grant me His favor on whatever I lay my hands on for His sake so that His Kingdom will be furthered through my efforts. I also ask Him to impress on me and guard my heart from the distractions of the world that could take my eyes off of Him so I can do more for Him and nothing against Him. As ministers, we are God's special representatives. God has personally chosen you and given you the privilege of serving Him. Never forget that the calling to serve God is a special honor. You have been chosen to serve the King of Kings. Never forget!

My biggest desire is to see students become committed followers of Jesus Christ, well beyond their youth ministry years. They face a difficult road ahead. We all do. We will encounter difficult times in ministry, and we may ask ourselves, "Why are we doing this?" That question is especially difficult when we see students continue to struggle to stay true to their commitments to Christ. I fully understand that it is only God who can change a heart, but it is still difficult to watch a student fall away from a once strong and committed relationship with Christ, usually when they begin their college years. To help students avoid falling away, I want to do everything in my scope of influence to enable them to experience Christ. I want them to experience Him through relationships, service, worship, and every other area of their lives. I always go back to the fundamentals of my youth ministry calling. They remind me that it is not by my abilities or strengths that lives are changed—Christ alone has the power to change lives. My responsibility is to love and serve Him faithfully and train others to do the same. For this reason, I give them the keys and watch them drive!

CPSIA information can be obtained
at www.ICGtesting.com
Printed in the USA
BVOW09s2313271217
503691BV00003B/217/P